TRANSFORMED

BY LOVE

LEIF HETLAND

ISBN: 978-1-942306-07-8

DEDICATION

To my baby girl, Katherine Nicole, who is God's amazing
love–gift to her family and to the world. May you forever
live a life of transforming love!

CONTENTS

Forward

In the movie, "Saving Private Ryan," two touching scenes brought me to tears. The first was when Private Ryan, finally found, knelt before the man who was dying in front him. He had led the team that had gone through many near-death struggles to find Ryan, protect him and get him home to his mom, who had lost all her other sons in battle. The last words of the dying hero were in answer to the question that had to do with how the young private could ever live up to the honor he had been paid by his dying benefactors. Two brief words comprised the answer, "Earn it."

The next touching scene takes us to a cemetery years after the war is over and Private Ryan, now an old man, approaching the grave of his benefactor, almost falling on the grave but righting himself, turned to his family and asked, "Have I been a good man?" In other words, "Have I loved well enough to be worth dying for?"

This book had to be written and Leif Hetland was the one to write it. Many can speak of love with great emotion and describe, in passionate tones, its power and worth. To be honest I get more out of a few seconds of a clear-cut demonstration of love than from a whole series of sermons on the subject. Leif was the one to write this volume on this grand theme, not because of his studies on love or because he can stir the emotions of his hearers (which he can) but because he speaks and lives and loves with intentionality and relentlessness. And his life speaks more loudly than his voice. He has learned to love unconditionally and stubbornly refuses to allow anything or anybody to steal his love.

Leif is a long-standing son who models to me and all who watch him the power of pure and relentless love. He loves everyone but seems to wind up loving most the last, the lowest, the least and the lost. He has made the choice and will not turn back. This same message you read here will appear in months to come with more love sightings, more miracles of changed lives and a clearer path for us to walk in step together to prove that "Love never fails, always wins we can do it too!"

Thanks, Leif for practicing what you preach! It looks good on you.

Jack Taylor
Dimensions Ministries
Melbourne, Florida

Introduction

I have long considered myself a student of the love of God. I have traveled all across the world, seen many kinds of peoples, and many kinds of cultures. The one constant, the one thing that crosses all barriers, translates in all languages, and overcomes all resistance, is the love of God.

His love covers a multitude of sin. His love is patient. His love is kind. His love is the final authority over all mankind. His love is the completion of our salvation. His love is the reason. His love is our hope. His love is always pointed at us.

I share this book as a declaration of love. It is a testament of how passionate His love is for His people, how hungry He is to release His love, and how far His love is willing to go. I hope that, in reading this book, you find yourself in a deeper place of connection with His love, inspired to share His love with others, and ready to embrace His love as it begins to cover every part of the earth.

I have included personal application activities at the end of each chapter. These are not arbitrary exercises, but tools to begin stretching your capacity to experience the love of

God. It is my sincere hope that you take these lessons of love out of the book and into your life. I believe that we are in a season of unprecedented potential harvest. All we need are the eyes to see what God has laid out before us. I have designed every personal application to train your body and soul to recognize the love of God in your life and in the lives of others.

Finally, I hope that you will not read this book alone. Your heavenly Father is with you and always has been. He is ready to speak His words of love directly to your heart, more clearly and profoundly than the hand of any writer could. Be listening to Him. He is ready to begin transforming your life with His love, so that you can partner with Him and transform the world.

PART ONE

LOVE TRANSFORMS US

*"If we want God's love to transform the world, then we must first
let it transform us."*

CHAPTER ONE

THE UNSTOPPABLE FORCE

I recently decided to pay a visit to my home country of Norway. I usually only have time for meetings and conferences when I visit, but this time I made sure to set aside some time to reacquaint myself with my home town. I thought it would be fun to stop by my old elementary school. Most of what had been there back in my day was gone or renovated to the point of unfamiliarity. However, I noticed a hill nearby and at that moment I began to reminisce. Though the hill was bare now, I remembered a big tree that used to stand at the top of it.

I saw myself sitting under that very tree when I was eight years old. I remembered the loneliness as I sat there, sucking my thumb. It was a habit I had yet to break, and the other children made sure to let me know how babyish they thought it was. I sat under the tree, watching the other children play with a growing sense of shame and embarrassment swell in my chest. I wanted to play, but I was afraid of what they would say. I was just a "thumb sucking baby" after all, why would they want to play with me anyway? Before the feelings of longing and anxiety could bring me to tears, I felt an unexpected warmth fill my heart. Although this feeling was completely new to me then, it was a warmth that I would become very familiar with in the later parts of my life.

The warmth drew my eyes upward to small clusters of sparkling lights that danced among the many colored leaves above. This sense of warmth didn't get rid of the bullies or the names they called me, but as I looked at these swirling particles of light I somehow knew I was not alone.

This was only the first of many memories that came as I revisited my childhood. I remembered harsh words spoken by teachers or other students, but I also remembered that warm presence being there. I remembered feeling overwhelmed by schoolwork, but the presence was there as well. I remembered all the painful and challenging circumstances of my young life. That warm, peaceful presence was there for each and every one.

I then began seeing later parts of my life. The presence was there even when I chose to use drugs to try and fill the hole in my heart, offering its true fulfillment in place of the false one the destructive substances offered. The presence was there even as I ran away from God, choosing to pursue darkness because of fear and pain.

Even in this season of darkness and rebellion, that warm presence continued to pursue my heart. I remember being called into the principle's office during high school. The meeting started with a lengthy lecture outlining how perfect my older sister had been during her time at this school. The principal compared her perfect attendance, excellent grades, and compliant attitude to my record of declining grades, rebellious action, and drug use. The comparison only served to make me feel a sense of shame that drove me deeper into the dark places of my heart, but then the principal's tone changed.

He then spoke of the potential he saw in me. He said I was a young man with the ability to influence hundreds even thousands. He told me that I could be a force of good in the world. Though my young heart was still too closed off to receive all that he was saying, I felt that warm presence on every word.

Then more memories came. I saw the day I was delivered from darkness into light, when I finally stopped running and accepted Jesus as my Lord and Savior. I saw how I traded running from God for running after God. Then I saw how I became misguided in my pursuit, feeling that I needed to perform to earn my Heavenly Father's favor. I did not realize that the love I was striving to earn had been with me long before I would have even known how to pursue it. I saw the day I was delivered for the second time, from religion to sonship. In that moment I finally connected with the warmth that had been following me all of my life.

Moment by moment, memory by memory, God was revealing the lifelong pursuit of His love toward my heart. Tears filled my eyes as the memories came, faster and faster, big moments and small ones. I had known, of course, that I had found his love when I was first saved. I even knew the change that came when I stopped working *for* love and started working *from* love. Despite knowing all this, I had no idea just how relentless his pursuit had been.

I didn't have the language or the knowledge to recognize His love when it first visited me, so I had not seen it for what it was. Now, having spent years of my life serving from the knowledge of His love, I was seeing my entire life in a brand new light. It changed my perspective on everything, nothing was the same.

God's love is an unrelenting force, an unyielding and unending river of purest goodness that does not grow tired and does not grow weak. It is not a placid lake that waits calmly only for those willing to seek out its shimmering shores. God's love moves throughout the Earth, seeking any and all methods of entry into every heart, open or shut. It is not a limited resource, doled out conservatively so that each may have their fair share. It is without limit and without end. He is ready to pour it all out on anyone and everyone, and there is nothing that can stand against it.

Romans 8:38-39 says:

> *38 For I am convinced that neither death nor life, neither angels nor demons, neither the present nor the future, nor any powers, 39 neither height nor depth, nor anything else in all creation, will be able to separate*

us from the love of God that is in Christ Je-
sus our Lord.

Truly nothing can separate us from God's love. There is no sin, no shame, no thought, no pain, no doubt, no fear, and no failure that can stop God's love from pursuing us. I thought I knew this, I thought I knew it well, but as the Lord took me through memory after memory, revealing just how relentless his love had been, I saw it with new eyes. It is one thing to know the love of God, it is another to see it working in your life day after day, moment after moment.

This love is the most powerful force in the universe. It is capable of turning darkness into light, freeing captives, healing all diseases, transforming cultures, redeeming kingdoms, and restoring relationships, but it must start from within each one of us. Because what good is it if we transform the world but are not also transformed ourselves?

Lost and Found

There once was a man with two sons. His younger son came to him one day and said, "Father, I do not wish to work for you any longer. I wish to have the full measure of my inheritance, as if you had died."

Though it saddened the man that his son no longer wished to be with him, the man gave his son what he desired.

Soon after, the young man gathered all his new wealth,

along with all his belongings, and traveled to a far off place. There he spent all he had on extravagant parties and all the other earthly pleasures money could buy. Naturally, this lifestyle could not be maintained for long.

The wealth, which seemed so vast when he left his father's estate, was suddenly and completely gone. To make matters worse, a famine struck the country where he now lived. Desperate and out of options, he took the only job he could find, feeding pigs for a local farmer. This barely covered his living expenses. Food prices were extremely high because of the famine, so he hardly had anything to eat. It got so bad that, before long, the pig slop began to look tasty.

It was then that the young man was struck with an idea. Even my father's lowliest servants have plenty to eat, he thought. I'll go back and beg my father for a job. I've given up my rights as a son, but maybe he will accept me as a worker.

Back at the estate the father sat waiting, as he often did these days, watching the place where the road crested over hill, hoping to see a figure walking up the lane back to his house. Though each day was met with disappointment, he did not give up his vigil. Finally, after what seemed like a lifetime, the figure he had been waiting for came trudging along the road. The young man was more ragged and thin than when he had left, but the father recognized him instantly.

The father dropped what he was doing and sprinted down the lane to meet his son. The young man opened his mouth to begin his carefully rehearsed apology, but was immediately struck silent as his father collided with him. The impact was so strong that the young man nearly fell over, but he was held steady as his father wrapped him in his arms and pulled him close. Again the young man tried to confess his failures as a son, but his father kissed him on the face again and again.

Finally the young man was able to squeeze in the first part of his apology, "Father I am no longer to be called your son, I have sinned against heaven and against you-" but before he could say any more, his father held up a hand to silence him.

The father turned to one of his servants, who had just managed to catch up, and said, "Quick, bring my best clothes. Put a ring on his finger and new shoes on his feet. Prepare all the best food, open all the best stock we have been saving, and call everyone. It is time for a celebration," he then turned and directed the last part of his instructions while gazing directly at his son as tears fell down along his cheeks, "For my son was dead, but now he is alive again. He was lost, but now he is found."

Later that night, as the celebration began, the father noticed that his older son was nowhere to be seen. After hearing from one of his servants that his older son had decided to not attend the party, the father went outside to meet with him.

Outside, the older son stood with arms crossed, his face red, and a thick vein pulsing on his neck. Ignoring this, the father asked, "What's wrong? Why haven't you come to the party?"

The older son let out a steamy sigh and said, "I have

served you for my whole life, always doing what you say and never going against you."

The father nodded. He knew all this to be true.

The son continued, steadily losing the grip on his temper, "Have I ever been thanked for the way I work for you? No! But when my brother, who disgraced the family name and directly rejected you, returns from squandering the fruits of your generosity, you throw him the biggest party I've ever seen."

"My son," the father stepped forward and put a hand on his older son's shoulder, "you are always with me, and everything I have is yours. I would have thrown you a party any time you wanted. But now your brother has returned. He was dead, but now he is alive again. He was lost, but now he is found."

Prodigal or Prudent

The story of the prodigal son is, perhaps, the most well known of all Jesus' parables. Many consider it to be a picture of God's willingness to receive all into His kingdom, no matter how far their sin has carried them from Him. While this is true, I believe this is a very limited view of all that is revealed through this story. It is a story of how relentless God's love is for his children, and it is a cautionary tale of how easily that love can be missed or ignored.

Some of us have been like the younger son. We've run from God and sought out the best the world has to offer.

After we discover that there is no lasting satisfaction to be found in worldly pursuits, we return to our father.

Others are more like the older son. We never leave our father's house, serving him with all diligence and honor. We slave away, doing all we can to earn our inheritance, to avoid being like our foolish brother. We think that this is the more prudent path, but, as we see at the end of Jesus' parable, the result is disconnection with the father.

I have been both sons at different point of my life. First I was the younger son. Because of fear and pain I ran from God, seeking pleasure wherever I could find it. I spent most of my adolescence in a cycle of fleeting satisfaction and consistently growing emptiness. Finally I had my own moment "feeding the pigs" and decided to return to my father's house. However, in my zeal to overcome my history as a prodigal son, I became like the prudent son.

Like the older son I strove to earn my birthright. Every aspect of my life had to be perfect. I had to have a certain number of attendees at my church. I had to preach a good enough message. I had to know the word better than anyone else. I felt insulted when someone younger and with less experience than me would teach a powerful message. I asked the Lord a question similar to the one the older son asked his father, "Where is my deep revelation? I have served you with all my heart and you give *them* your words to share?" My striving fostered a spirit of competition and performance that killed all the joy in my life and made me forget the first love I found when I was a prodigal son.

Maybe you are a prodigal son right now. You have been running from God, searching to find all the pleasure you hope exists in the world. Or perhaps you are a prudent son. You strive every day to follow the rules of your father's house. You grit your teeth and resist temptation when it comes. You go to every church meeting, volunteer for every church outreach, and read your Bible every day. While there is certainly nothing wrong with any of these things, they do not guarantee that you are truly living in God's love.

Whichever son you more closely match, we all need to be wary of missing the love that God has to release on each one of us. Whether we are running from it or running for it so fast that we miss that it's right in front of us, none of us can afford to miss God's love. We cannot bring the change we wish to see in the world until we live in a constant knowledge of God's love for us. First we must recognize which path we are more likely to stumble down, the path of the prodigal or the path of the prudent.

The Prodigal Son

The younger son misunderstood the value of his relationship with his father. He saw their relationship as a means of acquiring wealth and wealth as a means of acquiring pleasure. Because of this he took what he could get and went out into the world, looking to be fulfilled by all the pleasures therein.

While it is likely that most of you reading this book are not fully running away from God, it is still possible that you are searching for pleasures that can only be found through relationship with Him. Do you ever think, *once I start making enough money I'll feel better, I just need to find the right person to marry,* or *once I find the right job everything will be fine.*

Though God wants to give you the desires of your heart, we are being fooled if we think any of those things will satisfy us forever. That ever-flowing river of satisfaction can only come from the heart of God. The amazing part is that from that place of relationship with Him, things like money, a healthy marriage, and the right job come much more easily.

Some may think that we stop being a prodigal son the moment we enter God's kingdom. In truth, we always have the option of going out on our own to chase the desires of our heart, but if instead we choose to stay in our father's house we will learn how to obtain those desires in a way that no famine can take away.

The Prudent Son

The older son's mistake was not recognizing all that was available through his relationship with his father. While the younger son took all that he could from his father, the older son never asked for anything. This could be perceived as more admirable at first glance, but in truth it was just as much of a mistake as that of his younger brother.

The father said it himself, "You are always with me," and, "all I have is yours." God expects us to have desires. He wants to see our dreams fulfilled. Most of them were placed in our heart by His own hand. Denying this out of a false sense of humility so that we may be more judicious servants will only serve to set us on the path to exhaustion and disappointment.

We are not slaves, but sons and daughters. Good sons and good daughters serve their parents, but they are also not afraid to share their desires and dreams. And God has said that we are his children as in Galatians 3:26-29:

> *26 So in Christ Jesus you are all children of God through faith, 27 for all of you who were baptized into Christ have clothed yourselves with Christ. 28 There is neither Jew nor Gentile, neither slave nor free, nor is there male and female, for you are all one in Christ Jesus. 29 If you belong to Christ, then you are Abraham's seed, and heirs according to the promise.*

We rob ourselves when we try to earn, through diligent and faithful service, that which God wishes to give us by birthright. It suppresses our dreams and stifles our ability to feel and experience God's love.

The Love is Already There

I was shocked when God revealed the legacy of love that lay hidden in my own history. Though I had seen it when I was saved from drug abuse and again when I was saved from the fruitless treadmill of religion, I had never known how constant His pursuit of my heart had been.

The love was always there. The love that has now grown so familiar in my heart was always with me. Every moment His love was pursuing me, and every moment His love is pursuing you. This love, this unrelenting force, will continue pursuing you for the rest of your life. It doesn't stop when you start knowing and experiencing it, because God's love is infinite! There is always more and more and more.

To transform the world, to bring change to every place on this planet, we need to first become so full of His love that we spill over. Only from this place of overflow can we transform cities and nations. Otherwise we too easily fall into strife.

Personal Application

Below I have included the original version of the "parable of the lost son" found in Luke 15:11-32. Read through it and begin asking the Lord to reveal how His love as followed you all the days of your life. Don't be afraid of the hard moments or seasons that may be in your history, He is neither afraid or ashamed of them. His love is more powerful than anything. It can transform any situation for good.

11 Jesus continued: "There was a man who had two sons. 12 The younger one said to his father, 'Father, give me my share of the estate.' So he divided his property between them.

13 "Not long after that, the younger son got together all he had, set off for a distant country and there squandered his wealth in wild living. 14 After he had spent everything, there was a severe famine in that whole country, and he began to be in need. 15 So he went and hired himself out to a citizen of that country, who sent him to his fields to feed pigs. 16 He longed to fill his stomach with the pods that the pigs were eating, but no one gave him anything.

17 "When he came to his senses, he said, 'How many of my father's hired servants have food to spare, and here I am starving to death! 18 I will set out and go back to my father and say to him: Father, I have sinned against heaven and against you. 19 I am no longer worthy to be called your son; make me like one of your hired servants.' *20 So he got up and went to his father.*

"But while he was still a long way off, his father saw him and was filled with compassion for him; he ran to his son, threw his arms around him and kissed him.

21 "The son said to him, 'Father, I have sinned against heaven and against you. I am no longer worthy to be called your son.'

22 "But the father said to his servants, 'Quick! Bring the best robe and put it on him. Put a ring on his finger and sandals on his feet. 23 Bring the fattened calf and kill it. Let's have a feast and celebrate. 24 For this son of mine was dead and is alive again; he was lost and is found.' So they began to celebrate.

25 "Meanwhile, the older son was in the field. When he came near the house, he heard music and dancing. 26 So he called one of the servants and asked him what was going on.27 'Your brother has come,' he replied, 'and your father has killed the fattened calf because he has him back safe and sound.'

28 "The older brother became angry and refused to go in. So his father went out and pleaded with him. 29 But he answered his father, 'Look! All these years I've been slaving for you and never disobeyed your orders. Yet you never gave me even a young goat so I could celebrate with my friends. [30] *But when this son of yours who has squandered your property with prostitutes comes home, you kill the fattened calf for him!'*

[31] *"'My son,' the father said, 'you are always with me, and everything I have is yours.* [32] *But we had to celebrate and be glad, because this brother of yours was dead and is alive again; he was lost and is found.*

Questions to Ponder

Are you more like the prodigal son or the prudent son?

Do you have desires that distract you from pursuing a deeper relationship with God?

What would it take for you to trust that God wants to see all your desires fulfilled?

Are there dreams or desires in your heart that have grown stale?

What would it look like to start pursuing those dreams tomorrow?

CHAPTER TWO

FACE TO FACE

Several years ago I was sharing at a conference in South Hampton, England. Randy Clark, Bill Johnson, and several others were sharing at the conference as well. I had heard through the grapevine that Bill's assistant, Judy Franklin, had a strong gift for releasing people to encounter God in a new way. I didn't hear too many details about how she went about doing this exactly, but several of my friends insisted that I go and have her pray for me. I decided that I would do just that, since many of them had had a wonderful experience with her ministry.

So I spoke to Bill and arranged the meeting, and soon found myself in a small side room above where the conference was being held. Judy and I sat in the middle of the room. She asked me to close my eyes and started giving me small things to begin picturing in my minds eye. Even as she began to speak, my mind filled with richly detailed images, creating a sudden and vibrant scene.

I saw myself walking down a well-laid cobblestone path. A beautiful stone wall paralleled the path to my right, while the left side was lined with rows of thick and healthy looking trees. Though all of this was happening in the confines of my own mind, I could vividly sense the smell of the fresh grass, the feel of the cool air, and the light sound of bees as they moved from flower to flower.

The old Baptist pastor that still lived somewhere down inside me kept insisting that this was simply an example of "divine imagination," my own mind interpreting and expressing the things of God in a metaphorical manner. Yet another part of me was certain that this was all quite real, perhaps even more real in some ways than the chair I was sitting in.

Judy continued with her prompting, "Now you're coming to a doorway. Do you see it?"

I nodded, for as she spoke I saw myself come to a free-standing doorway in the middle of my path.

"Alright," Judy said, "Go through the door, it leads to a park."

And sure enough, it did. I found myself in the middle of a beautifully landscaped park. A small waterfall fed a stream that wove its way in and out between green hills and thriving oak trees. The sun sat at the perfect spot, sending sparkling light shimmering across the surface of the stream and accenting every curve and bend of the trees.

"Do you see a bench?" Judy asked.

It was just then that I did, over a small bridge to my

right, near the waterfall.

"Go sit on the bench and then invite Jesus to come sit with you."

So I made my way to the bench, listening to the trickling sound of the waterfall, and sat down on the soft and well worn wood. Both in the vision and in the small side room at the conference center, I took in a deep breath and asked aloud, "Lord Jesus, would you please come and sit with me here today?"

There was a momentary pause, and then He came. My heart leapt as I saw Him approaching down the same path from where I had come. Though I could easily see every detail about His hands, feet, and body, His face was obscured.

My mind raced as He approached. The old Baptist pastor kept insisting that this was all in my own mind, an accurate picture of Jesus' desire to connect with me, but just a picture. However, I couldn't deny the sense of wonder I felt at the sight of Him. This didn't feel like a vision. It felt real.

Despite this uncertainty, all my thoughts fell silent as Jesus sat next to me on the bench.

"What would you like to ask me?" He said.

Hundreds of questions flooded my mind. When are you coming back? Why didn't I get healed after my back injury? What is going to happen with the church over the next ten years? How can I lead more people into your presence? They all filled my mind, each piling on top of the last, dozens and dozens of curious thoughts all fighting to be first in line.

It felt as though several minutes went by as I sat there stumbling over my own thoughts. Finally, my mind settled, and the biggest question emerged from the depths of my heart and rose to the surface.

Turning to Him I asked, "Jesus, have I loved you well?"

He did not answer right away. Instead He reached over and put His hand on my back. Every question in my heart was answered by that simple touch. Every thought was fulfilled by His affection. It was not simple information, not just a "yes." I *experienced* the love that flowed from His heart. It was a lifetime of affection packed neatly into the simplicity of a gentle touch.

Suddenly I found myself back in the small room, sitting in a chair with tears pouring down my face. I stayed there for a few moments as waves of emotion flooded over me again and again. Something deep inside had changed and it would never be the same again.

Though the change in my heart remained, I began to feel questioning thoughts enter my mind in the days after my encounter. Had it just been in my own mind? Was it nothing more than a simple vision? If so, then why had I emerged feeling so changed? Then I remembered 2 Corinthians 12:2, where the apostle Paul shared a brief story:

> *2 I know a man in Christ who fourteen years ago was caught up to the third heaven. Whether it was in the body or out of the body I do not know—God knows.*

With that scripture in mind, I decided that it didn't really matter if what I had seen was just a vision or an actual face to face encounter with Jesus. The impact on my life was undeniable, my hands still shake when I recall the way His touch felt on my shoulder. Was I merely experiencing a metaphorical expression of my own desire to love God, or had I experienced a true heavenly encounter with the Lord Jesus Christ? God knows and, until I do too, I choose to let the impact of the love I felt transform my heart and mind.

How Do We Get There?

Every Christian is meant to have a face to face encounter with God's glory. Not just read stories about His glory or hear testimonies about it, but to experience it first hand. The ministry of the Holy Spirit in our lives is meant to release us into a deeper encounter with His glory. Paul compared the laws of Moses to the ministry of the Spirit in 2 Corinthians 3:7-8 saying:

> *7 Now if the ministry that brought death, which was engraved in letters on stone, came with glory, so that the Israelites could not look steadily at the face of Moses because of its glory, transitory though it was, 8 will not the ministry of the Spirit be even more glorious?*

In other words, if laws of Moses, which were brought before the redemption of Jesus' blood, brought so much glory that Moses needed to hide his face from the Israelites, how much more glory should we expect now that we have been adopted into God's kingdom and have the Holy Spirit as our guide? Paul continues to unpack this idea in 2 Corinthians 3:16-18 saying:

> *16 But whenever anyone turns to the Lord, the veil is taken away. 17 Now the Lord is the Spirit, and where the Spirit of the Lord is, there is freedom. 18 And we all, who with unveiled faces contemplate the Lord's glory, are being transformed into his image with ever-increasing glory, which comes from the Lord, who is the Spirit.*

If we are in relationship with Jesus then our faces have been unveiled. We are free to experience His glory. In fact, this glory is meant to be part of our day to day walk with Him.

We cannot see the transformation we wish to see in the world until we see that same transformation in our own hearts. We cannot transform our hearts with good works, diligent study, or even through relationships with other people. All these things are certainly a part of the process, but all our transformation must start with a personal face to face encounter with God. We need to see the love in His eyes, feel the affection in His heart, and know the good thoughts He thinks about us. It is from this place of love that we are inspired to do good works, study the ways of God, and create healthy and fruitful relationships with others.

Now, every encounter will look different from person to person, and every encounter will look different depending on the season of your life. The vision I had after Judy prayed for me was not the first encounter I had with God's love and it certainly wasn't the last. I've encountered His love in the word; scriptures suddenly coming alive on the page, causing wave after wave of understanding to flood my heart. I've encountered it in my friendships; kind words in times of crisis or encouragement in times of growth. There is no limit to the ways our Father expresses His love to us.

For me there have been three keys that have helped to ready my heart for encounters with Him. They are simple, but His love is simple too.

First, don't let anything get in the way of encountering Him. If you don't have time, make it. Your work will get done faster if you are connected to His heart, you will have more energy to spend time with your family, and you will get new ideas and revelations about how to make your life more restful and efficient. It really doesn't take long to connect with God, but the effects will last a lifetime.

Second, don't let the lies of the enemy make you feel unworthy of God's presence. It doesn't matter what you've done in your past. It doesn't matter what you've done this morning. Flaws, sins, and issues of character are all better repaired in the presence of God than they are outside it. God saw every moment of your life and decided that you were worth saving. Nothing surprises Him. Even if you are angry at God, He is ready to meet with you. He is not scared of your questions or emotions. He is not a father that requires perfection in His presence. He is a father that will pull you onto His lap and gently wipe away all the blemishes and stains. Don't let the condemnation of the enemy scare you away from the very thing that will bring you freedom.

Third, simply pursue Him. All you need to do is show up and He will meet you there. This is not the time of Moses. You do not need to climb the mountain to get to the place His glory dwells. *"But whenever anyone turns to the Lord, the veil is taken away."* We need only turn to meet Him and there He is. Trust that your pursuit will not go ignored. He loves you and is excited to meet with you. *"And we all, who with unveiled faces contemplate the Lord's glory, are being transformed into his image with ever-increasing glory, which comes from the Lord, who is the Spirit."*

Personal Application

Now it is time for you to have your own face to face encounter with Jesus. Don't be afraid and don't be discouraged. Some find it easy to encounter God, for others it takes several tries. I don't know if I would have had the encounter I did if I had met Judy ten years earlier. We are all growing in our understanding of His goodness. Don't be discouraged, follow the wisdom of the old phrase, "If at first you don't succeed, try, try again."

First repeat this simple prayer aloud during your quite time with Him:

> *Jesus, I thank you for the sacrifice you made.*
> *That same sacrifice that allows me to approach you with boldness and faith.*
> *Please help me to be transformed by your love.*
> *Let me encounter your heart so that I might know you more.*
> *Make my heart and mind open to you.*
> *Teach me to follow your presence every day of my life.*
> *Thank you for making it possible for me to be close to you.*
> *Amen.*

Now I have included a simple guide to help lead you into an encounter similar to the one I had when Judy prayed for me. You may see something similar or you may see something completely different. You'll know that you've connected with Him when you feel the love, peace, and joy that only the spirit of God can bring.

*Picture a pathway through a beautiful
wooded area.
Walk down the path at whatever pace you
wish, but take your time.
There is no rush.
Soon you will come to a door.*

*The door leads to a special garden built just
for you.
No one but Jesus has seen this garden.
It is meant only for you and Him.
Spend some time in the garden.
Admire how perfectly it is made just for you.*

*When you are ready find a place to sit.
It can be on a bench, on a hill, under a tree,
or anywhere else you like.
Invite Jesus to come sit beside you.
Just wait, He will come.
Sit and speak with Him for a while.
He may have much to say, or maybe He just
wants to listen.
Stay until you are ready to go.*

Was that just a vision? Was it just your "divine imagination" revealing the desires of your own heart? Perhaps and perhaps not. God knows. What is important is that we practice meeting with God face to face. It's a big part of what Jesus died for after all.

Questions to Ponder

What questions would you ask Jesus if you could sit with Him for an hour?

How do you think your life would look different if you met face to face with Jesus every day?

What factors do you see hindering you from meeting with God every day? Time, relationships, stress, fear, a painful history?

What do you think it would take to remove those limitations?

CHAPTER THREE

LOVE ENCOUNTER

It was a hot day in the Samarian town of Sychar. A woman was making the long journey from her home to collect water at the town well, a daily ritual in arid lands like these. She had been late in completing her morning chores, so she hadn't been able to start her trek until the heat of the day was in full effect, a fact she was regretting more and more by the second.

The vessels she carried were heavy now and would be quite daunting on the way home when they would be full of water. She looked up and was grateful to see that the well was only a few more steps away.

Then she nearly dropped all her vessels as she noticed that a man was sitting near the well, a Jewish man. Though an outsider would likely be unable to identify the difference between a Samaritan and a Jew on first sight, hundreds of years of animosity between the two cultures made all the differences stand out like a sore thumb to those in either camp.

Knowing her place, the woman averted her eyes from the man that sat near the well. Who knew what would happen if the man thought she had been looking at him, or if they should accidentally meet eyes? The woman shuddered at the thought, speeding her work at the well, hoping to escape from the socially awkward situation as quickly as possible.

"Will you give me a drink?" the man's question resounded in the silence, though he had spoken it gently. The woman grew stiff, freezing with the filled vessel in her hand. This man, this Jewish man, had just spoken directly to her. Most Jews would never acknowledge the existence of a Samaritan man, much less a Samaritan woman. It just wasn't done. In fact, many Jews would refuse to even eat off a plate that a Samaritan had used.

Dozens of thoughts raced through her mind, until finally she decided that there was nothing to do but respond.

"You are a Jew and I am a Samaritan woman," she said with the tone of one who knows nothing better than to state the obvious, "How can you ask me for a drink?"

This seemed to amuse the man. He smiled and said, "If you knew the gift of God and who it is that asks you for a drink, you would have asked him and he would have given you living water."

"Sir," the woman continued, still dumbfounded that this conversation was even happening, "you have nothing to draw with and the well is deep. Where can you get this living water? Are you greater than our father Jacob, who gave us the well and drank from it himself, as did his sons and livestock?"

"Everyone who drinks from this water will be thirsty again," the man sitting by the well continued, "but whoever drinks the water I give them will never thirst. Indeed, the water I give them will become in them a spring of water welling up to eternal life."

There was something strange about this man, the woman thought. No one had ever spoken to her this way. Yes, he spoke in some kind of riddle, but there was no restraint in his voice. It was like speaking to an old friend. So she decided to play along with his riddle.

"Sir," she said, "give me this water so that I won't get thirsty and have to keep coming here to draw water."

"Go call your husband and come back," he said.

Her voice caught in her throat. She quickly forced out the first thing she could think to say, "I have no husband."

The man smiled at this, "You are right when you say you have no husband. The fact is, you have had five husbands, and the man you now have is not your husband. What you have said is quite true."

The woman fought to keep her mouth from hanging open. Again, she could do no better than state the obvious, "Sir, I can see you are a prophet." Something was welling up in the woman's chest. A question, a hope, deeper than the well that sat next where she stood. She had to know, but she was afraid to ask, so first she said, "Our ancestors worshiped on this mountain, but you Jews claim the place where we must worship is Jerusalem."

"Ma'am," the man replied, "believe me, a time is coming when you will worship the Father neither on this mountain nor in Jerusalem. You Samaritans worship what you do not know; we worship what we do know, for salvation is from the Jews. Yet a time is coming and has now come when the true worshipers will worship the Father in the Spirit and in truth, for they are the kind of worshipers the father seeks. God is spirit, and his worshipers must worship in the Spirit and in truth."

The woman knew what she must ask, but her hope had grown so much that she was now unable to ask it. So instead she hid it in a statement, "I know that Messiah is coming. When he comes, he will explain everything to us."

The man smiled and looked directly at her, "I, the one speaking to you, I am he."

An explosion filled the woman's chest. A joy that she couldn't contain. She left the full vessel where it lay and ran back to the town as fast as she could. Everyone had to know, she had to tell them all. Messiah had come. He was sitting by the well that their forefather Jacob had given to them.

Don't Miss Love When It Comes

I've always been fascinated by the story of the Samaritan woman who met Jesus by the well. The time and distance that lie between us and the stories found in scripture can sometimes dull their impact.

Jesus had been ministering all day and was on his way back to Galilee from Judea. He took the route through Samaria. This already was unusual, as many devout Jews would take the longer route around Samaria just to avoid running into any Samaritans. The history between Jews and Samaritans carried both religious and racial weight. Mutual animosity was deeply seeded in both cultures. Perhaps this is why Jesus used them as examples so often.

The differences between men and women were much more pronounced during this period of history. It would have been considered inappropriate for a man to speak to a woman he did not know while she was working at the well. It was unheard of for a Jewish man to speak to a Samaritan woman.

Despite all these cultural boundaries. Despite all the potential for offense or misunderstanding. The woman recognized Jesus for who he was. She not only opened the door for a personal encounter with Jesus, she opened the door for her entire town. Later in the story we see that many Samaritans ended up having an encounter with their savior, all because this one woman chose to believe.

I'm fascinated by this story because it reminds me of how delicate encountering Jesus can be. It wouldn't have taken much for this story to have gone completely different. What if the woman had been too embarrassed by Jesus' questions? What if she had seen a Jewish man sitting next to the well and decided that she would just come back later? What if she had let her social prejudices, or the prejudices she would have expected Him to have, prevent her from hearing the truth behind Jesus' words? It seems to me that her need to know Jesus was greater than her fear of social norms.

The Pharisees were put to the same test, time and time again. Christians like to poke fun at the Pharisees, and I understand why. It is easy to see how foolish they were to miss that their Messiah had come. However, I sometimes think that the story of the Pharisees is one of the most tragic in the Bible.

They had their Messiah. The one they had dedicated their lives to studying. They knew all the prophesies that foretold his coming. They likely knew every one by heart. Yet they missed the Messiah even as He stood in front of them. It can be easy to poke fun at them, but I would rather learn from them.

How Do We Recognize Love?

It can be frightening, seeing how easily and consistently the people that dedicated their lives to studying the Messiah missed Him when he came. If these master scholars were able to make such a huge mistake, then what hope does the average Christian have? Thankfully, we have the opportunity to learn from their mistakes. We can learn to avoid the traps that ensnared the Pharisees. I believe that there are three simple keys that can help posture our hearts to recognize and receive His love when it comes.

Be expectant, but don't have expectations. God's ways are mysterious. Sometimes my best times with Him are when I spend hours in my room worshipping, praying, and diving into the word. Sometimes my best times with Him happen during the ten minutes it takes to get to my office. Sometimes the best thing I hear from Him is a single word. Sometimes it is a rich and detailed vision. God likes variety and values unique expressions of His love.

If we expect Him to only show up in certain ways and at certain times, then we are likely to miss out when He shows up in a new way. If we expect the only way He speaks is in a loud and rushing storm, then we will miss the still, small voice. If we expect Him only to speak through the still, small voice, then we are likely to think it is a distraction when He comes and speaks through the loud and rushing storm. Expect Him to speak to you, but don't be surprised when it comes in an unexpected way.

Look for the fruit first. In can be disconcerting when God comes in a way that we have not experienced before. There have been great debates within Christianity over whether speaking in tongues, being "slain in the spirit," "holy laughter," spiritual gifts, and other such manifestations are legitimate expressions of God's presence. Many of these debates have lead to bitter arguments, church splits, or even the formation of new denominations. While I do think it is important to test all manifestations, I believe that we should test their fruit first.

If a gift or manifestation releases love, joy, peace, patience, kindness, goodness, faithfulness, gentleness, or self-control then I am much more likely to trust it.

I believe that testing everything by the letter of the law is what caused the Pharisees to mistrust and eventually betray Jesus. They rejected Him because He did not fit their exact interpretation of the Messiah. I think we do better when we keep our tests simple. Look for the fruit of the Spirit first.

Get to know God's heart, then get to know His ways. First we need to experience God, only then can we understand Him. Our God is living and relational. He is interested in a personal relationship with us, not a professional relationship. The only way we can understand what He does is to become familiar with His heart. To do this we must also be more interested in a personal relationship than a professional one. We must seek to understand who He is, not just what He can do for us.

The Pharisees made it their priority to analyze every detail of the law. They strove to bring clarity and specificity to every letter of the law. It is my opinion that this focus was the beginning of their downfall. When we forget the central purpose that lies behind everything that God does, when we forget that God is love, it becomes easy to miss the message behind the letter of the law. We fail to see the forest through the trees.

If we understand the heart of God, that everything He does is in service of love, then we can see how His word and His actions are all expressions of that same love. Otherwise we are likely to make the same mistake as the Pharisees and sabotage the savior we sought to serve.

Personal Application

There are many things that can limit our ability to experience God's love. We will be discussing many of them in subsequent chapters, but I think it is a good idea to start talking with God about this now. Being transformed by God's love is not always an instantaneous process. Some things change all at once, others can take a great deal of time. But I believe that we can shorten the time it takes by being intentional about softening our heart.

Read through the original account of Jesus meeting the Samaritan woman at the well, keeping in mind all the social, racial, and religious issues that could have lead to the woman missing her encounter with the Messiah.

As you read, ask the Lord to reveal any prejudices, hurts, or lies that would cause you to miss an encounter with Him. It is not my desire that you get overly introspective or get down on yourself. It is the Holy Spirit's job to reveal mindsets that need to be changed in you. And when He does it will not bring condemnation but freedom. That is how you will know it came from Him.

Once any of these lies or mindsets are revealed, ask the Holy Spirit which truths He wants to replace them with. He is so good at equipping us to receive His love.

John 4:4-26

4 Now Jesus learned that the Pharisees had heard that he was gaining and baptizing more disciples than John— 2 although in fact it was not Jesus who baptized, but his disciples. ³ *So he left Judea and went back once more to Galilee.*

⁴ *Now he had to go through Samaria.* ⁵ *So he came to a town in Samaria called Sychar, near the plot of ground Jacob had given to his son Joseph.* ⁶ *Jacob's well was there, and Jesus, tired as he was from the journey, sat down by the well. It was about noon.*

⁷ *When a Samaritan woman came to draw water, Jesus said to her, "Will you give me a drink?"* ⁸ *(His disciples had gone into the town to buy food.)*

⁹ *The Samaritan woman said to him, "You are a Jew and I am a Samaritan woman. How can you ask me for a drink?" (For Jews do not associate with Samaritans.)*

¹⁰ *Jesus answered her, "If you knew the gift of God and who it is that asks you for a drink, you would have asked him and he would have given you living water."*

¹¹ *"Sir," the woman said, "you have nothing to draw with and the well is deep. Where can you get this living water?* ¹² *Are you greater than our father Jacob, who gave us the well and drank from it himself, as did also his sons and his livestock?"*

13 Jesus answered, "Everyone who drinks this water will be thirsty again, 14 but whoever drinks the water I give them will never thirst. Indeed, the water I give them will become in them a spring of water welling up to eternal life."

15 The woman said to him, "Sir, give me this water so that I won't get thirsty and have to keep coming here to draw water."

16 He told her, "Go, call your husband and come back."

17 "I have no husband," she replied.

Jesus said to her, "You are right when you say you have no husband. 18 The fact is, you have had five husbands, and the man you now have is not your husband. What you have just said is quite true."

19 "Sir," the woman said, "I can see that you are a prophet. 20 Our ancestors worshiped on this mountain, but you Jews claim that the place where we must worship is in Jerusalem."

21 "Woman," Jesus replied, "believe me, a time is coming when you will worship the Father neither on this mountain nor in Jerusalem. 22 You Samaritans worship what you do not know; we worship what we do know, for salvation is from the Jews. 23 Yet a time is coming and has now come when the true worshipers will worship the Father in the Spirit and in truth, for they are the kind of worshipers the Father seeks. 24 God is spirit, and his worshipers must worship in the Spirit and in truth."

25 The woman said, "I know that Messiah" (called Christ) "is coming. When he comes, he will explain everything to us."

26 Then Jesus declared, "I, the one speaking to you—I am he."

Questions to Ponder

What do you expect God's love to look like as it begins to transform your life, how will it come?

Looking back, has there ever been a spiritual gift or manifestation that offended you or that you considered to be, "not of God"?

How do those experiences stand up against the "fruit test?" Did they release love, joy, peace, patience, kindness, goodness, faithfulness, gentleness, or self-control?

Are there any prejudices, hurts, or lies in your life that might limit your ability to experience God's love?

What would it look like if those were completely removed?

Ask the Holy Spirit which truths and kingdom mindsets He wants to give you in place of your prejudices, hurts, or lies. What did He show you?

PART TWO

LOVE TRANSFORMS OTHERS

"As we discover the magnitude of God's love for each of us, it is only natural that we begin showing that same love to those around us."

CHAPTER FOUR

SEEING THROUGH THE EYES OF LOVE

The short man sprinted through the crowded city streets, bumping his way through the throng as fast as his legs would take him. He was breathing hard and a stitch was tearing at his side. The great rabbi was coming through town, the one that some even dared to call Messiah.

Zacchaeus had never held much interest in the workings of the rabbi's. Great teachers came and went. The talk of this teaching or that teaching would peak and then decline, replaced by the teaching of some other great rabbi. The talk surrounding this man had been different. Zacchaeus first heard of his teachings. "The man speaks with authority," they were saying, "It is not the same as the other rabbi's. Perhaps this could be he, the messiah."

This was nothing out of the ordinary. They had been

under Roman rule for long enough that every upstart rabbi and street minister was thought to be the Messiah, at least for a while. The people were hungry to be saved from the oppression of Roman rule. Zacchaeus was a prudent man. He knew better than to jump up at the first mention of "messiah."

He was surprised, however, when the talk did not stop. "He's healed a man of leprosy and cast demons from two others. I heard he fed a whole crowd with nothing more than a few fish and loaves. The old blind man in the square, the rabbi prayed for him and now he can see."

Talk of this new teacher only grew in scope and magnitude. Even the jaded old tax collector had to take notice. Then Zacchaeus heard that the rabbi would be coming though Jericho. Though he had a sudden thrill on hearing the news, he wasn't sure if it would be wise to go see the rabbi. Zacchaeus was a tax collector, he collected money and goods on behalf of the Roman empire, the oppressors of his own people. Surely any man claiming to be the Messiah, the savior of the Jews, would view him as a traitor.

But all the stories he had heard, how could he not go see the man that had all of Israel talking? It certainly couldn't hurt to at least get a look at the man. He finally decided to go at the last minute, and discovered that, despite his reservations about how the rabbi would react to the presence of a tax collector, he felt the need to run so as not to miss him.

The crowds seemed to be growing thicker. It was getting harder and harder for Zacchaeus to keep up his pace. Finally he made it within a few feet of the road. He knew the rabbi must be close because he could hear people shouting for him.

Zacchaeus had never been a tall man. Even standing on his toes and straining his neck he was unable to see past the thick group of people that crowded around the teacher. Somewhere during the run, his casual interest had turned into a desperate need. He had to at least see the rabbi's face.

Zacchaeus tried wiggling between a small gap between two broad-shouldered men, but there was no use. The crowd was simply packed too tight. The desperation to see the teacher growing in his chest, Zacchaeus began to panic, searching desperately for some way to get through the crowd. His eyes darted from left to right, finding no gaps or spaces to push through, then his eyes drifted upward.

A thick-branched sycamore tree sat off to one side. The crowd around it was loose, broken up by the uneven ground that had been displaced by the thick roots of the tree. The tree was a little bit further from where Zacchaeus thought the teacher was, but one of the branches looked low enough for him to reach. And, judging by the movement of the crowd, it was not too far from the path the teacher was following.

He ran toward the tree, ignoring the pang of embarrassment at how ridiculous a man of his age and social standing would look clambering up a tree like a child. He grabbed the lowest branch with a leap and hefted himself up with no small effort. It took every bit of concentration to keep from slipping as he climbed. He settled partway up a thick branch, gripping it with one hand while he held the other out in an effort to maintain his precarious balance.

"Zacchaeus."

He froze, shocked by the sound of his own name. Keeping a firm grip on the branch, he looked down to see who had called him.

The man who called his name stood just below him. He had no particularly distinguishing features. Zacchaeus doubted he would have been able to pick him out of a crowd under normal circumstances. However, the crowd was clearly surrounding the man who had called his name. There was something more too. Something Zacchaeus couldn't put his finger on. Could this be-

"Zacchaeus, come down from there," the teacher said, "I must stay out your house today."

Zacchaeus didn't know what to say other than, "Of course."

In a daze, the tax collector slid down from the tree and led the teacher, along with the majority of the crowd, back toward his house.

Zacchaeus' mind was racing. The teacher had known his name. Surely if he had known that then he would know what Zacchaeus did for a living. He would know that he served the very people that oppressed the ones the rabbi came to save. He would know that Zacchaeus was paid more if he collected more. He would even know of all the tricks, manipulations of the law, and outright lies that he had used to accumulate his great wealth.

Despite this, the teacher had called him by name and asked to be a guest in his house. It was the most honoring thing a visiting rabbi could have done. And he did it to Zacchaeus, the tax collector.

He could hear the crowd muttering their reproach, even

as he and the teacher entered his house. "He goes to the house of a sinner," they were muttering. But this was nothing new to Zacchaeus. He knew what the people of his city thought of him, he had grown accustomed to their scorn. What he hadn't been prepared for was the unashamed honor that the teacher had shown to him.

Something began to stir in Zacchaeus' heart. Part of it felt something like guilt, but it was much more than that, something deeper, more profound. It wasn't shame, that was a poison he was all too familiar with. No, this carried none of the paralyzing ache of shame. He felt empowered. He knew what he had to do.

Later, at dinner, Zacchaeus stood, addressing the rabbi and the crowd, "Look Lord! Here and now I give half my possessions to the poor, and if I have cheated anybody out of anything, I will pay back four times the amount."

A gasp shot through the crowd, but it was quickly silenced as the teacher opened his mouth to speak, "Today salvation has come to this house," the next part he addressed to the crowd, "because this man too, is a son of Abraham," then the great teacher looked directly into Zacchaeus' eyes, "For the Son of Man came to seek and save the lost."

Loving the Unlovely

The story of Zacchaeus is extremely powerful. Tax collectors were not just disliked during Jesus' time, they were reviled as the scum of the earth. Roman authorities quickly learned that appointing tax collectors from within the local community netted significantly greater profits than sending in a Roman official. People could more easily hide their wealth from an outsider, but a member of the local community would have a clearer idea of how much each person had. Tax collectors were given a commission based on how much money they were able to bring in, so they were encouraged to get as much as they could by any means necessary.

Zacchaeus was apparently good at his job, because he is called "wealthy" in Luke 19:2. He would have been well known in the community, even infamous. Jesus' response to Zacchaeus would have been considered revolutionary. Not only did he honor a man who was both a thief and an oppressor, he chose to enter the man's house. At the time, entering the house of a known sinner would make Jesus "ceremonially unclean."

This is such a dramatic prophetic picture of the transformative power of God's love. Jesus made no attempt to correct or reprimand Zacchaeus for his actions. He simply honored him with his presence. What was Zacchaeus' response to this honor? Almost immediate repentance and restoration for all he stole.

We have all heard this story. We teach it to our children and sing songs about it in Sunday School. But I think we often forget to put the principle and perspective of the story into action. Our lack of cultural perspective hinders our ability to bring it to a modern context. It is essential that we learn to also love the unlovable people of our time.

Seeing Past the Junk

I was on a trip in Nampula, Mozambique several years ago. It was unbearably warm. People milled the streets while shop keepers hawked their wares. Tourists were looking for their illusive souvenirs. In every alley lurked the possibility of another thief.

An older gentlemen that was digging through a heap of what looked like garbage caught my eye. After a few moments he bent over, evidently finding what he was looking for. From the pile of junk he pulled out a twisted hunk of wood, to me it didn't look much different from anything else in the garbage pile. A look of excitement cut across his face. Curious about why he found this piece of wood so fascinating, I followed him to his make-shift shop. It was a small hut on the edge of the village. He sat down on an old stool in front of his home, and I watched as he pulled out a knife and began to carve at the twisted piece of wood.

It was slow work, but I was so curious about what he was making that I told the man that I would be back in one week to see what he had made. By the time I returned a week later, he was just putting the finishing touches on his piece of work. Out of that twisted and dirty piece of wood he had carved a beautiful piece of art. It depicted a collection of people—men, women, and children—all knitted together in an intricate wooden latticework.

I immediately purchased the piece from the man, paying more than he was asking. I was sure that God was telling me something. Later, back at the hotel, the Lord spoke to me about what had happened, "You saw junk, but the wood carver saw people. You saw nothing of value, he saw everything the wood could be."

Our God is a fountain of everlasting hope. There is no case that is to hard for Him. I could see no potential in that grungy piece of wood, it didn't even look like it would make good firewood, but the craftsman saw what I could not. God, the great craftsman of heaven and earth, can see the potential that we are unable to see. We must learn to transform our perspective. We must learn to see the world as He sees it, even in the most extreme cases.

Modern Tax Collectors

On December 11th, 2008 Bernard Lawrence Madoff was arrested on suspicion of securities fraud. It soon came to light that Bernie Madoff had, over the course of multiple decades, built his investment company into one of the biggest financial scams in history. Thousands of clients were affected. Many still have not recovered from the loss. Billions of dollars were missing and everyone wanted answers.

Bit by bit the details became clear. Madoff had lured in new clients with conservative, but still impressive promises about what his firm could do with their investments. As new clients came in, he would use their money to pay the expected revenue of older clients. It was a cycle that was doomed to fail since, eventually, more clients would be wanting to cash out than the new clients coming in could cover. The result was a massive expectation of profit where, in fact, there existed none. This amounted to almost sixty-five billion dollars.

People were angry, disappointed, and hungry for justice. But what does justice look like? Madoff was sentenced to ten years in prison, forced to forfeit the seventeen billion that he did have, and left with no hope of being restored to his career or possibly any career. Is that justice?

This is a hard question. Bernie Madoff undoubtedly caused tremendous pain and financial strain with his massive scheme. But does his suffering bring restoration to those who were affected?

What would Jesus have said to Bernie Madoff? We've seen how Jesus reacted to the tax collector Zacchaeus. Was Madoff's crime all that different?

Now I know what you're thinking. Zacchaeus confessed his crimes and promised to repay those he cheated. Bernie Madoff only confessed when he was about to be found out. The pressure of his scheme had grown so large that he would have been caught soon. Plus he wasn't able to pay back his debts, there wasn't enough money.

Luke 19:3 tells us that Zacchaeus was just coming to "see who Jesus was." There is no implication that he had any desire to turn from his wicked ways until after Jesus called his name and honored him with His presence. He was transformed by Jesus' love.

I don't know all the right answers when it comes to criminal justice. I don't know if it's right that a man be locked away for ten years and have everything taken from him. What I do know is that things would have gone differently if Bernie Madoff had met Jesus. What if he had met Jesus when he was studying finances in school? What if he met Jesus the day he opened his first investment business? How would things be different?

We are Christians, translated literally this means "little Christs." We are Jesus' representatives. Running into us should be like running into Jesus. We must learn to react to people, and the injustices they sometimes cause, the same way that Jesus would.

Bernie Madoff made a big mess, but what about the people in your own life that make smaller messes? What should you do if a pastor is caught skimming money from the church? What do you say to a friend who starts earning money through dubious means? How do you treat the teenager that shoplifts from the local grocery store?

Jesus did not condone Zacchaeus' actions, in fact He shared a parable about managing money in a godly manner shortly after meeting with the tax collector. But He treated him with honor. Though Jesus had every right to condemn Zacchaeus, instead, He went to dinner at his house.

If we truly want to bring lasting transformation to the world, then we need to learn to look past injustice and love the unjust. Only by bringing the love of God to the unjust can we hope to bring heaven's justice to the earth.

Personal Application

It is hard to deal with injustice. Anger, fear, disappointment; all these are normal responses when we see injustice in the world. We are meant to approach the problems of the world from a higher perspective. We must learn to view the world with the perspective of love.

Now I am going to ask you to think of someone that committed an injustice in your life. It can be big or small. Use the first one the Holy Spirit brings to mind. While thinking of that person and that situation, I want you to pray this simple prayer:

Jesus, help me to see (insert person's name) as you see them
I give you my anger, my fear, and my disappointment
I give up my right to justice
Trusting that you are the one who will bring justice
Teach me how to forgive
Teach me how to trust
So that I can treat others the way you would

Now, with that prayer still in your heart, read the original story of Zacchaeus. Keep the cultural perspective of the time as best as you can. This man had stolen from his neighbors and countrymen for his own profit and the profit of their oppressors. He had cheated honest men out of their fair wages. From this perspective, imagine how unexpected

Jesus' response would have been. Receive an impartation of Jesus' ability to look from the perspective of love.

Luke 19:1-10

> *1 Jesus entered Jericho and was passing through. 2 A man was there by the name of Zacchaeus; he was a chief tax collector and was wealthy. 3 He wanted to see who Jesus was, but because he was short he could not see over the crowd. 4 So he ran ahead and climbed a sycamore-fig tree to see him, since Jesus was coming that way.*
>
> *5 When Jesus reached the spot, he looked up and said to him, "Zacchaeus, come down immediately. I must stay at your house today." 6 So he came down at once and welcomed him gladly.*
>
> *7 All the people saw this and began to mutter, "He has gone to be the guest of a sinner."*
>
> *8 But Zacchaeus stood up and said to the Lord, "Look, Lord! Here and now I give half of my possessions to the poor, and if I have cheated anybody out of anything, I will pay back four times the amount."*
>
> *9 Jesus said to him, "Today salvation has come to this house, because this man, too, is a son of Abraham. 10 For the Son of Man came to seek and to save the lost."*

Now, as a way of exercising your capacity for honor, I want you to write a letter to your spouse or a close friend. Make it a letter of affirmation and encouragement. Say only the things you love and value about them. Try to honor, through words, the gifts of God you see in their life. Pack as much love and kindness as you can into the letter. Do not fluff it out with meaningless compliments, look for the real and substantial good in their lives. Then give the person the letter and see what effect it has on them.

After that, if you feel up to it, you could try writing a similar letter to the person who you prayed about in the previous exercise. Learning to see the people that wrong us through the eyes of God is a powerful step toward becoming more like our maker. If we are to truly love the unlovely as Jesus did, then we need to start where it is most personal.

Questions to Ponder

What are some of the injustices you have seen committed in your life?

What would it look like for heaven's justice to invade those situations?

How could you show honor to the people who have committed those injustices?

Are there people that you have a hard time seeing through the "perspective of love?"

What do these people have in common? Are they all wealthy, part of a certain political association, or from a certain denomination?

What are you going to do to ensure that your heart is always open to the love God has for others?

CHAPTER FIVE

A CHOSEN VESSEL

In the town of Damascus there lived a disciple of Jesus named Ananias. It was a difficult time to be a follower of Jesus Christ. Jesus had been crucified, raised from the dead, and ascended to heaven. The influence and size of Christianity was growing rapidly, and this made the current religious leaders nervous. The chief priests had appointed men to travel throughout the land, hunt down the members of this new religion, and silence them by any means necessary.

Alone in his home, Ananias heard the call, as he had so often, of the Lord's voice.

"Ananias!" the Lord called.

"Yes, Lord," he answered.

"Go to the house of Judas on straight street and ask for a man from Tarsus named Saul, for he is praying. In a vision he has seen a man named Ananias come and place his hands on him to restore his sight."

Ananias felt a chill run down his spine. He knew who Saul of Tarsus was, every Christian in the region knew. Saul was one of the most ruthless and efficient agents of the chief priests. He had already arranged the stoning of several key church members, and was rumored to be coming to this part of the country looking for prisoners to bring back to Jerusalem.

"Lord," Ananias tried to measure the tone of his response, "I have heard many reports about this man and all the harm he has done to your holy people in Jerusalem. And he has come here with authority from the chief priests to arrest all who call on your name."

"Go," the Lord responded without hesitation, "this man is my chosen instrument to proclaim my name to the Gentiles and their kings and to the people of Israel. I will show him how much he must suffer for my name."

A vision filled Ananias' mind as the Lord spoke. He saw the man Saul riding with his companions down the road to Damascus. A sudden and bright light flashed before the men. The men fell to the ground, struck by the sudden release of power. His companions looked this way and that, unable to see where the light was coming from, but Saul's eyes remained fixed at the very center of the light.

Through the vision, Ananias could see that the Lord Jesus had appeared to Saul. He could not hear what was being said, but Ananias knew the words of his Lord well enough to make a good guess.

Though he was still afraid, Ananias knew that the Lord was doing a great work in Saul's life. He had learned to trust the voice of God more than his own instincts, and so he left his house quickly, and soon found himself at the doorway of the house.

Inside he saw the man Saul laying in the middle of the room. All the anxiety he felt on the short journey to the house melted away. He knew what he must do.

"Brother Saul," he said, putting his hands on the man's head, "the Lord – Jesus, who appeared to you on the road as you were coming here – has sent me so that you may see again and be filled with the Holy Spirit."

Then something like scales fell from Saul's eyes, and immediately his sight was returned.

Transformation

Saul later became the man known as the Apostle Paul. He saw numerous miracles, started many churches, and was, in many ways, single handedly responsible for the spread of the gospel to the Gentiles. He would go on to write a great deal of the New Testament and disciple several other great leaders of the faith.

What would have happened if Ananias hadn't been obedient to the word that the Lord gave him? What if he had done the prudent thing, and hidden away from the man who had killed and captured so many of his brethren? Surely the credit for Saul's conversion belongs to the Lord, He did knock him right off his feet after all, but God decided to have the remainder of Saul's transformation be led by one of His disciples.

Saul was a hard case. He was not just indifferent to Jesus, he actively sought to destroy His followers. He was not content to debate the differences he had with Christianity, he wanted to crush it to dust.

It is easy, because we have the benefit of knowing the extent of the rest of his ministry, to minimize the severity of Saul's origins. However, we can see in Ananias' initial reaction to God's word that Saul was a man to be feared. He was so consistent and strong in his belief that the chief priests, who were working tirelessly to undermine the spread of Christianity, entrusted him with their authority. This would give him the right to search people's houses, interrogate whomever he pleased, and take prisoners to be tortured and questioned back in Jerusalem.

Saul was a violent and ruthless religious zealot. Yet still God chose him to be his vessel, his instrument. How far is God's love willing to go?

How Far Will Love Go?

On September 11th, 2001 the mindset of Americans changed. We were shocked by one of the most devastating attacks in the history of the country. Two thousand nine hundred and ninety six people died in just a few minutes. A radical religious group claimed responsibility shortly after.

What was your response? Anger, fear, sorrow? Many didn't know what to do. What would Jesus' response have been?

More recently, terrorist groups calling themselves ISIS have been waging a campaign of hatred and violence throughout the middle east and further.

What is your response? What is God's response?

If God can transform the life of the violent religious zealot, Saul, then why can't He transform the life of a modern day terrorist?

There once was a terrorist named Ahmad. Ahmad was a suicide bomber, sent to kill infidels with a payload of liquid explosives. Ahmad was successful in his mission. Everything had gone according to plan except for one small detail, Ahmad survived.

He awoke in an American military care center, badly burned and barely alive. He was surrounded by people he couldn't understand. He had been told that the Americans would torture and humiliate him – that he would be imprisoned for the rest of his life if he were ever caught. His experience turned out to be quite different.

The doctors and nurses attended to his every need, they eased the pain of his burns, fed him regularly, and spoke to him in gentle and consoling tones. Though he couldn't understand anything that was said, the intent was clear. They were taking care of him.

Ahmad had a long and painful recovery, but later said that the kind care of the doctors and nurses made that time far less painful than his cruel upbringing. He left the care center with a plan to learn English and visit America. He now dedicates his time to educating young Muslims against the path of terrorism. He now follows a path of peace, all because a few military doctors treated him with kindness and dignity.

God's love has no limits. No matter what damage has been done, His love can bring restoration. No matter how much hate tries to get in the way, His love is stronger. He is not afraid of any terrorist. He can see the young boys and girls that are hidden deep inside. He can see how they were taught to live from hate and fear. Love is stronger than hate. Where there is love there is no room for fear and God's love covers a multitude of sin.

We must learn to see even the most extreme evil in the world from the perspective of God's love. It is the only way to bring the change we wish to see in the world.

I saw one of the most profound examples of this at a conference I shared at recently. I had been sharing about the power of God's love and the transformation it was bringing to the Muslim communities I had visited.

A family approached me after the meeting. It was a husband and wife with two small children. As they approached, I noticed that the wife was leading her husband by the arm. It only took one look at his face to see why. All the visible skin on his hands, neck, and face was covered in scars. One of his eyes was missing, leaving behind only a flat pocket of scar tissue, while the other eye stared blindly to one side.

He told me about how, during his tour of duty, his unit had been attacked with an improvised explosive device. The blast had blinded and nearly killed him. He then reached out his hand. In it was a check for a thousand dollars.

"I want you to use this to bring the love that you are talking about to the people that did this to me," he said, "I want them to experience the love that God has for them."

I was stunned. How could this man, who had suffered so much at the hands of those who despised him, find enough forgiveness in his heart to hope that the people that had maimed him would know the love of God. If that was not enough, he was also willing to make a huge sacrifice to ensure that this love would reach those dark places.

We are called to love our enemies and bless those who curse us. It may be costly, it may take a massive amount of forgiveness, but the results will inspire everyone to invite more of God's love into their lives.

What Can I Do?

Jesus himself showed up to meet Saul with the "right hand of fellowship" and began the transformation of Love in his life. However, Ananias was clearly the next step in God's plan. His obedience gave Saul another push in the direction of becoming the Apostle Paul. Would Saul have become Paul if Ananias had decided to ignore God's direction? We will never know. Perhaps God would have sent another or perhaps Saul would have never recovered from his blindness.

It can be daunting to look at the problem of terrorism, but the solution is simple and starts in your own life. Ananias did one simple thing to help Saul along his path to becoming Paul. He obeyed.

Fear always tries to steal our love. It scares us away from the risk of evangelism. It scares us away from praying for the sick. It scares us away from stepping out in the prophetic. It even scares us away from sharing our hearts with the people that care for us.

We need to learn to trust in the power of God's love. It covers a multitude of sin. It can make up for our faults and limitations. All we have to do is give it a chance. You don't have to start with terrorists. Start by loving the homeless people in your community. Love the atheists. Love the Buddhists. Love the Muslims. Love the Hindus. Love the Catholics. Love the Protestants. Don't let there be anything that puts a cap on the love that flows from your life.

Love, real love, can only come from God. All of us were made to be like our Father, so all of us are built to recognize love. Even the ones who have become full of hate. Show God's love wherever you go and I guarantee that you will see people respond to it.

A long time ago I was facing one of the hardest things I had faced in my life. It was a Wednesday night in the church we attended in Alabama. The pastor at my church wanted people to be praying for me during this hard season, so he asked me to stand before the congregation and share that I had become addicted to pain killers during my recovery from a horrific car accident several years before.

I sat in the pew, tapping both feet, knowing that he was going to invite me up at any moment. Honestly, I wanted to take more pills just to escape the shame that I was feeling. I wanted to hade from the sorrow I caused my family, the response of the congregation, everything.

In two days I was going to check into a treatment center in California. This meant that I would be missing the family trip back to Norway. I insisted that my wife and children still go on the trip. They would do better being comforted by my family than sitting at home worrying about me.

My wife and I sat in the front pew. I felt like a death row inmate awaiting execution. Though, I thought grimly, that an execution would be swift and painless. The process I was about to go through would be long and hard.

As I sat there with my head hanging between my knees, I saw a pair of two large feet step out in front of me. I looked up and saw the six foot tall frame of my son, Leif Emmanuel. He reached out his hand and pulled me to my feet. Then he wrapped his arms around me and pulled me into the biggest, strongest bear hug I had ever had.

He said, "I love you," then returned back to his seat.

I sat back down, still feeling the warmth of the embrace on my chest. My wife, Jennifer was bawling next to me.

She looked at me and said, "Do you know what he just did?"

I looked back, confused.

"Do you understand?" she asked again, "Really, do you?"

I shrugged, confused.

"He just walked all the way from where he was sitting with his friends, knowing full well what was going to happen, pulled you to your feet and said he loved you in front of God and everyone else."

We all have moments when we are in desperate need of God's love. Sometimes this is because our own mistakes or faults. Sometimes this is because of the choices of others. Regardless, we all find ourselves in that place from time to time. Just as you hunger to receive love in those situations, remember that you may be the one carrying God's love during someone else's situation. You may be the light in the darkness, just as my son was for me during that dark moment of my life.

It would be easy to see how me son could be upset or disappointed with me. Instead, he decided to release his love. And now that moment has lived with me for the rest of my life. Love in a place of brokenness is often the most sweet.

Personal Application

Now it's time to put your love into action. Love is of little use as a theory. Love is meant to be done, not just said. Repeat this prayer:

*Jesus teach me how to love without limit and
without restraint.*
Teach me to see others as you do.
*Show me the people you want to love and how
to love them.*
*Show me how to ignore the fear that would try
to keep me from showing love.*
*Show me how to love even the most extreme
hard cases*
Show me how to love them just as you would
Amen.

Find a place to sit quietly and speak with the Holy Spirit. There is someone in your life right now that needs to hear about God's love. It could be a complete stranger or someone you've known for a long time. It could be a devout Christian or someone who has never heard Jesus' name. It could be someone who has hurt you or it could be someone who has been kind to you. But there is someone.

Ask the Holy Spirit how He wants you to show His love to them. Maybe it could be as simple as a small gift. Maybe it will be a word of encouragement. Maybe it is the gift of time and company. Maybe it is just a hug. Just wait, He will show you how to love them.

Now, go and do it right away. Don't talk yourself out of it. This is a chance to make sure that fear does not limit your ability to show God's love to others.

Here is the original version of Saul's conversion. Read it and think about what it would look like for God to bring this kind of transformation to some of the hard cases that you know.

Acts 9:1-19

> *1 Meanwhile, Saul was still breathing out murderous threats against the Lord's disciples. He went to the high priest 2 and asked him for letters to the synagogues in Damascus, so that if he found any there who belonged to the Way, whether men or women, he might take them as prisoners to Jerusalem. 3 As he neared Damascus on his journey, suddenly a light from heaven flashed around him. 4 He fell to the ground and heard a voice say to him, "Saul, Saul, why do you persecute me?"*
>
> *5 "Who are you, Lord?" Saul asked.*
>
> *"I am Jesus, whom you are persecuting," he replied. 6 "Now get up and go into the city, and you will be told what you must do."*

7 The men traveling with Saul stood there speechless; they heard the sound but did not see anyone. 8 Saul got up from the ground, but when he opened his eyes he could see nothing. So they led him by the hand into Damascus. 9 For three days he was blind, and did not eat or drink anything.

10 In Damascus there was a disciple named Ananias. The Lord called to him in a vision, "Ananias!"

"Yes, Lord," he answered.

11 The Lord told him, "Go to the house of Judas on Straight Street and ask for a man from Tarsus named Saul, for he is praying. 12 In a vision he has seen a man named Ananias come and place his hands on him to restore his sight."

13 "Lord," Ananias answered, "I have heard many reports about this man and all the harm he has done to your holy people in Jerusalem. 14 And he has come here with authority from the chief priests to arrest all who call on your name."

15 But the Lord said to Ananias, "Go! This man is my chosen instrument to proclaim my name to the Gentiles and their kings and to the people of Israel. 16 I will show him how much he must suffer for my name."

17 Then Ananias went to the house and entered it. Placing his hands on Saul, he said, "Brother Saul, the Lord—Jesus, who appeared to you on the road as you were coming here—has sent me so that you may see again and be filled with the Holy Spirit." 18 Immediately, something like scales fell from Saul's eyes, and he could see again. He got up and was baptized, 19 and after taking some food, he regained his strength.

Questions to Ponder

Is there anyone in your life that you would consider a hard case like Saul was?

What would it take for love to transform their life?

Have you ever been prompted to show God's love to someone and then didn't because of fear?

What could you do differently next time?

Think of the person you would have the hardest time showing love to, it can be someone you know or someone you've heard of. Ask God how He would show love to them. What did He say?

CHAPTER SIX

STRONGER THAN DEATH

Martha struggled to hold back the wave of tears that was forming in the corner of her eyes. There had already been so many tears, what good would more do? She had to be strong, for her sister's sake at least. Mary never had the steadiness that came naturally to Martha. Her sister would need all the support she could get during this trying time.

Mary sat on the far side of the room, head in her hands, tears flowing freely. This only solidified Martha's desire to hold back her own sorrow. She had to be strong.

Several people had made the journey from Jerusalem to the town of Bethany where the sisters lived, bringing what comfort and condolences they could. One of these, Martha wasn't sure of his name, entered the room and approached her.

"He's here," was all he said, but Martha knew exactly who he meant. She looked over at Mary who looked up for a moment, but quickly returned her face to her hands, lost in another bout of sobbing.

"I'll go see him first," Martha said, touching her sister lightly on the head as she exited the room.

So he's here, Martha thought as she made her way out of the house. How long had it been since she sent word for him? Six days? Seven maybe. It was hard to remember now. She had lost track after… after his timely arrival no longer mattered.

She saw him standing in the road, a small crowd already forming around him. Despite the depth of sorrow that clawed at her insides, she couldn't help but give a little smile at the sight of him. She approached, but the momentary gladness was snuffed out as she remembered how long it had taken him. How, if he had only been a little faster…

"Lord," she spoke to him as respectfully as she could manage, holding back a fresh wave of sobs, "If you had been here," she choked, tears streaming down the sides of her face despite her best efforts, "if you had been here my brother would not have died." She felt like a child, so unlike herself. She tried to make up for this by saying, "But I know that even now God will give you whatever you ask."

Jesus answered, confidence and peace saturating every word, "Your brother will rise again."

Despite herself, Martha rolled her eyes, "I know he will rise again in the resurrection at the last day."

"I am the resurrection and the life," more of that confidence and strength, "The one who believes in me will live, even though they die; and whoever lives by believing in me will never die." He looked her directly in the eye, "Do you believe this?"

"Yes, Lord," the tears flowed freely down her face now, all pretense of strength now gone, "I believe that you are the Messiah, the Son of God, who is to come to the world."

"Go fetch your sister," he said, "I would like to speak with her as well."

Though she loved being near him, Martha was grateful for the task. Anything to take her mind off the pain in her heart.

She found Mary where she left her, sobbing in their room. She, again, rested her hand on her sister's head and said, "The teacher is here and is asking for you."

Mary hopped up so suddenly that Martha took a little step back. Then, without another word, her sister marched out of the room and out the door. Martha quickly followed her, afraid that she might actually say something harsh to the teacher. However, as soon as Mary came face to face with Jesus she fell at his feet, slipping into yet another bought of sobs.

"Lord," Mary said, her voice cracking between her weeping, "if only you had been here, my brother would not have died."

Others began to weep when they saw the severity of Mary's sorrow. Even, Martha noticed, the teacher began to look troubled.

"Where have you laid him?" Jesus asked.

Several of the mourners answered at once, pointing in the direction of the grave. Jesus followed the crowd to the tomb, a small cave with a large rock placed to cover the entrance.

Suddenly, as he approached the grave, Jesus wept. Martha was shocked and, by the sound of it, so was the rest of the crowd. Some were moved by the teacher's show of emotion, "See how he loved him," they said. Others were skeptical saying, "Could not he who opened the eyes of the blind man have kept this man from dying?"

Martha wasn't sure how she felt. She had been sure that, once she sent word to Jesus, her brother would recover from his illness, but instead his condition only worsened. Then he died. She quickly counted on her fingers. That had been four days ago. Four days. What could have taken Jesus so long? The messenger had already returned, confirming that Jesus knew how dire their situation had become. Was the teacher delayed? Did he make stops along the way? Surely these would be important, she had no doubt about that, but could anything be more important than her brother's life?

"Take away the stone," Jesus spoke suddenly and with authority.

Yanked abruptly out of her own thoughts, Martha blurted out, "But, Lord, by this time there is a bad odor, for he has been there four days," there was a slight sting in the last two words.

Jesus turned to her and said, "Did I not tell you that if you believe, you will see the glory of God?"

Biting back tears, Martha looked him in the eyes and nodded.

A few strong men heaved the stone away from the entrance. Jesus looked back to the opening and said, "Father, I thank you that you have heard me. I know that you always hear me, but I said this for the benefit of the people standing here, that they may believe that you sent me."

Martha held her breath.

In a booming voice Jesus said, "Lazarus, come out!"

Immediately, a figure emerged from the darkness of the cave. He was wrapped, head to toe, in strips of linen, but even from where she stood she could see him moving underneath the fabric.

Laughing, Jesus said, "Take the grave clothes off and let him go."

Dealing With Disappointment

Sometimes things don't go the way we expect them to. Businesses fail, ministries fall apart, relationships become damaged beyond repair, and people die. Disappointment can come from many different places, but the result is often the same, a lack of hope. Hope is the joyful expectation of good. It is getting excited about what God has planned for your future, and expecting that future to be good.

I admire both Martha and Mary in this story. Neither of them tried to hide their disappointment from Jesus. They were honest with their feelings and told Jesus how they felt. "If only you had been here then my brother would be alive."

Too often, as Christians, we feel the need to be perfect in the presence of our creator. I imagine that this has a lot to do with the kind of perfection that we seem to require from each other in church settings.

"How's everything going?"

"Just fine. How about you?"

"We're doing great. Praise the Lord."

"Praise the Lord!"

I hear this conversation, or something like it, fifteen times every Sunday at church. Now, I'm not saying that there is anything wrong with being cheery. My problem is when someone tells me "We're doing great," and later I find out they are on the verge of divorce with their wife, they just lost their job, or their daughter just got kicked out of rehab. When we clog the arteries of the body of Christ with "I'm fine," and, "Everything's great," then there is no room for His life's blood to flow between us.

Mistakenly, we attribute this same need for everything to be "fine" to God. We feel that we are not permitted to tell God that we're disappointed or angry, especially if that anger or disappointment is directed at Him. Considering that God knows every thought you will ever have long before you have it, I find our lack of vulnerability with Him to be completely pointless.

How can we deal with the disappointments of life unless we share them with our heavenly father? How can we hope to find solutions and put them into action if we don't share those same disappointments with or spiritual brothers and sisters?

Mary and Martha knew Jesus well enough to be honest about their disappointment. Jesus did not scold them for their subtle reprimand or even their lack of faith. Instead He reminded them of who He was.

We don't need to hide our disappointments. Hiding them under a smiling mask will only cause our wounds to fester. Hiding them behind blind faith will only deepen their effects. We need to be honest with ourselves, each other, and God. Then God will have an opportunity to remind us of who He is, and that will build our faith.

In 2 Corinthians 12:9-10 Paul says:

> *9 But he said to me, "My grace is sufficient for you, for my power is made perfect in weakness." Therefore I will boast all the more gladly about my weaknesses, so that Christ's power may rest on me. 10 That is why, for Christ's sake, I delight in weaknesses, in insults, in hardships, in persecutions, in difficulties. For when I am weak, then I am strong.*

If we are afraid to show our weaknesses then how can God's power made perfect in us? God is not afraid of your disappointments or weaknesses, and He is not afraid of anyone else's either.

Healing the Brokenhearted

It is important to let the Lord lead us through the process of disappointment into renewed faith. How else will we know how to lead others there?

Many of the people that we see as unreachable hard cases are nothing more than broken-hearted people looking for wholeness. Whether they be as dramatic as billion dollar thieves or international terrorists, or as simple as a lonely man on the side of the road; everyone is searching for love. Some get more lost along the way than others, but their internal plight is the same.

Everyone is one encounter away from knowing the love of God; from the fear mongering terrorist to the self-righteous old religious Christian. It only takes one touch from His presence, one meeting with someone carrying the authority of heaven, to transform their lives forever. But first we need to have that encounter for ourselves.

We may feel that we need to appear perfect to the people we minister to, just as we sometimes feel we need to appear perfect to our fellow Christians. In truth, there is no shame in showing our humanity. Even Jesus wept at the tomb of Lazarus. Rather than alienating others, our vulnerability invites them in. People are much more attracted to a place where they can be themselves then a place where they have to be perfect.

Personal Application

Being vulnerable isn't always easy, even being vulnerable with God. However, vulnerability sets the table for love. Without it, love only has as much room as our hurts and disappointments allow. Now we are going to practice being open and vulnerable with God. Don't forget, He already knows everything you are going to say. But you must say it for your own benefit. Only then will there be room in your heart for what He has to give you. Say this prayer aloud:

Father, thank you for loving me without restraint.
Thank you for saying "yes" to me even knowing
every mistake I would make.
Help me to be honest and open with you, so that I
can also be open and honest with others.
I know this will bring me freedom and bring
freedom to many others.
Help me give you my pain and disappointments, so
that I may show others to give them to you too

Now, once again, find a quiet place and speak to the Father about any pains or disappointments you have in your life. They could be fresh, or situations from a long time ago. He's not afraid to bring old things up if needed. Speak your true feelings to Him, but know that He loves you more than anyone or anything else could. He is ready to start a journey of restoration that will bring healing to your heart and the hearts of anyone who crosses your path.

After you speak with Him, read through the original version of the resurrection of Lazarus. Be thinking of the emotions at play. Ask yourself, "Why did Jesus delay in coming to their aid?" and "Why did Jesus weep?"

John 11:1-44

> *1Now a man named Lazarus was sick. He was from Bethany, the village of Mary and her sister Martha. 2 (This Mary, whose brother Lazarus now lay sick, was the same one who poured perfume on the Lord and wiped his feet with her hair.) 3 So the sisters sent word to Jesus, "Lord, the one you love is sick."*
>
> *4 When he heard this, Jesus said, "This sickness will not end in death. No, it is for God's glory so that God's Son may be glorified through it." 5 Now Jesus loved Martha and her sister and Lazarus. 6 So when he heard that Lazarus was sick, he stayed where he was two more days, 7 and then he said to his disciples, "Let us go back to Judea."*
>
> *8 "But Rabbi," they said, "a short while ago the Jews there tried to stone you, and yet you are going back?"*
>
> *9 Jesus answered, "Are there not twelve hours of daylight? Anyone who walks in the daytime will*

not stumble, for they see by this world's light. *10* It is when a person walks at night that they stumble, for they have no light."

11 After he had said this, he went on to tell them, "Our friend Lazarus has fallen asleep; but I am going there to wake him up."

12 His disciples replied, "Lord, if he sleeps, he will get better." *13* Jesus had been speaking of his death, but his disciples thought he meant natural sleep.

14 So then he told them plainly, "Lazarus is dead, *15* and for your sake I am glad I was not there, so that you may believe. But let us go to him."

16 Then Thomas (also known as Didymus) said to the rest of the disciples, "Let us also go, that we may die with him."

17 On his arrival, Jesus found that Lazarus had already been in the tomb for four days. *18* Now Bethany was less than two miles from Jerusalem, *19* and many Jews had come to Martha and Mary to comfort them in the loss of their brother. *20* When Martha heard that Jesus was coming, she went out to meet him, but Mary stayed at home.

21 "Lord," Martha said to Jesus, "if you had been here, my brother would not have died. *22* But I *know that even now God will give you whatever you ask."*

23 Jesus said to her, "Your brother will rise again."

24 Martha answered, "I know he will rise again in the resurrection at the last day."

25 Jesus said to her, "I am the resurrection and the life. The one who believes in me will live, even though they die; 26 and whoever lives by believing in me will never die. Do you believe this?"

27 "Yes, Lord," she replied, "I believe that you are the Messiah, the Son of God, who is to come into the world."

28 After she had said this, she went back and called her sister Mary aside. "The Teacher is here," she said, "and is asking for you." 29 When Mary heard this, she got up quickly and went to him. 30 Now Jesus had not yet entered the village, but was still at the place where Martha had met him. 31 When the Jews who had been with Mary in the house, comforting her, noticed how quickly she got up and went out, they followed her, supposing she was going to the tomb to mourn there.

32 When Mary reached the place where Jesus was and saw him, she fell at his feet and said,

"Lord, if you had been here, my brother would not have died."

33 When Jesus saw her weeping, and the Jews who had come along with her also weeping, he was deeply moved in spirit and troubled. 34 "Where have you laid him?" he asked.

"Come and see, Lord," they replied.

35 Jesus wept.

36 Then the Jews said, "See how he loved him!"

37 But some of them said, "Could not he who opened the eyes of the blind man have kept this man from dying?"

38 Jesus, once more deeply moved, came to the tomb. It was a cave with a stone laid across the entrance. 39 "Take away the stone," he said.

"But, Lord," said Martha, the sister of the dead man, "by this time there is a bad odor, for he has been there four days."

40 Then Jesus said, "Did I not tell you that if you believe, you will see the glory of God?"

41 So they took away the stone. Then Jesus looked up and said, "Father, I thank you that you have heard me. 42 I knew that you always hear me, but I said this for the benefit of the people standing here, that they may believe that you sent me."

43 When he had said this, Jesus called in a loud voice, "Lazarus, come out!" 44 The dead man came out, his hands and feet wrapped with strips of linen, and a cloth around his face.

Jesus said to them, "Take off the grave clothes and let him go.

Questions to Ponder

How do you usually deal with disappointment?

How has your method of dealing with disappointment been working out for you?

How might an act of terrorism or criminal act be the result of a broken and disappointed heart?

How did Jesus respond to the disappointment expressed by Mary and Martha?

PART THREE

LOVE TRANSFORMS THE WORLD

"Soon, receiving love from God and showing that same love to others becomes a normal part of everyday life. It is then only a matter of time before His love permeates every part of society."

CHAPTER SEVEN

THE AUTHORITY OF LOVE

Some years ago, there was a treatment clinic in a small town. The clinic was responsible for treating people with various mental disabilities, some from genetic diseases or other ailments, others from drug abuse.

The clinic was well managed. The nurses enjoyed their work and had a genuine desire to see their patients get well, even lead normal lives someday. So, naturally, the clinic was very successful. Their success resulted in more and more patients being sent to their facility. Soon the modest campus became overcrowded. The doctor in charge of the clinic didn't want the patient's quality of life to suffer, but he also didn't want to turn any of them away.

One of the nurses came up with a solution. All they had to do was buy up some of the houses near the clinic. That way they could let some of the more healthy patients live outside the facility, only returning for treatment and checkups. It would solve their overcrowding problem as well as begin the process of integrating the healthier patients back into normal society.

Thinking that their worries were at an end, the head doctor took this plan to the town commissioner. Unfortunately the commissioner was not entirely convinced that the doctor's plan would work. Would people want mental patients for neighbors?

The commissioner called a town meeting. The head doctor outlined the clinic's plan, and almost immediately he could see that it was not going over well. People were grumbling and whispering to each other.

"It wouldn't be safe for our children to go out at night!" one man shouted.

"The crime rates would rise," said another.

The objections came like a flood after that, one piling on another. The head doctor hung his head, certain that his plan would be voted down. He would have to start thinking about which patients he could turn away.

Then, a hunched old woman began hobbling up toward the commissioners desk. She stood at the front of the room, raising herself up a little to reveal her kindly and wrinkled face.

She spoke softly and only shared a few words, but the weight of each syllable was undeniable to all who listened. Those near the front of the room noticed tears in her eyes as she said, "Please, oh please don't reject God's children."

Immediately, half the room began bursting into tears.

Even the old commissioner was weeping. The motion to allow the clinic to go through with its plan was unanimously approved. It wasn't until after that the town discovered that the old woman that had changed their hearts was, in fact, Mother Teresa.

No Weakness in Love

It is possible to feel powerless as a Christian in modern society. Political parties are full of corruption on all sides. Wars and rumors of wars fill every corner of the earth. Divorce rates continue to climb. Church leaders are regularly caught in adultery. How can we, the ones who are supposed to "turn the other cheek" and be as "gentle as doves" hope to bring change to the world?

1 Corinthians 13:4-8

> *4 Love is patient, love is kind. It does not envy, it does not boast, it is not proud. 5 It does not dishonor others, it is not self-seeking, it is not easily angered, it keeps no record of wrongs. 6 Love does not delight in evil but rejoices with the truth. 7 It always protects, always trusts, always hopes, always perseveres.*
>
> *8 Love never fails...*

It did not say love is weak. It did not say that love is powerless. It did not say that love is afraid. Many of the miracles Jesus performed were done when He was "moved by compassion." Love releases the power of heaven on earth. Love is aggressive. It seeks to bring the justice of heaven to every injustice on earth. It fights for the restoration of the victim and the redemption of the victimizer. God is love. Therefore love is powerful.

God's love sent His son to die for the redemption of all mankind. His love is the final authority in heaven and on earth. There is nothing higher.

I believe that the enemy has tried to rob love of its power. He wants us to feel powerless when confronted with the darkness in the world. In reality, we have been given all authority through the power of His great love.

We Are Commissioned

Jesus did not come just to die for our sins. If that were the case the Gospels would have been much shorter. Jesus came as the redeemer of our sins, but also as an example of what it looked like to be a child of God. His life was not just an act of love, it was an example. As He ascended into heaven, after He had been resurrected, He gave us a great commission:

> Matthew 28:18-20
> *18 Then Jesus came to them and said, "All authority in heaven and on earth has been given to me. 19 Therefore go and make disciples of all nations, baptizing them in the name of the Father and of the Son and of the Holy Spir-*

it, 20 and teaching them to obey everything I
have commanded you. And surely I am with
you always, to the very end of the age."

We have been commissioned with the full authority of heaven. Our words and actions are meant to carry that same authority. We are not meant to look at the pains and darkness in the world and be terrified. We are to look at it with the authority of kings and queens in the kingdom of God. We are to look at the world as ambassadors of heaven, commissioned to make our world look like His.

Personal Application

It is easy to see the darkness in the world, but we are called to something higher. We are called to be the light. We are called to be the city on the hill that cannot be hidden. We are called to shine. God's love acts both as the power to make us shine and the authority to let us do it.

Now let's attack the fears that have held us back from showing God's love to others. Whether it's as simple as not knowing where to start or as big as being overwhelmed by all the darkness we see in the world, God is ready to empower the church to do His work on the earth. If you need boldness, He will give it. If you need wisdom, He will give it. If you just need permission, He will give it. Pray this prayer:

Jesus, help me to see the world as you did when you were here.
Help me to not me overwhelmed, but inspired by what I see.
Show me how to release your goodness into the earth by the authority of your love.
Thank you for commissioning us with your authority.
Show me the tools you've given me to do your will.

With that in mind, read the testimony of the seventy two that were sent by Jesus. These were not the twelve disciples, just people that wanted to follow Jesus and walk in His ways. Be listening to the Holy Spirit. He will start telling you the ways He is going to release the transformative power of His love through your life.

Luke 10:1-24

1 After this the Lord appointed seventy-two others and sent them two by two ahead of him to every town and place where he was about to go. 2 He told them, "The harvest is plentiful, but the workers are few. Ask the Lord of the harvest, therefore, to send out workers into his harvest field. 3 Go! I am sending you out like lambs among wolves. 4 Do not take a purse or bag or sandals; and do not greet anyone on the road.

5 "When you enter a house, first say, 'Peace to this house.' 6 If someone who promotes peace is there, your peace will rest on them; if not, it will return to you. 7 Stay there, eating and drinking whatever they give you, for the worker deserves his wages. Do not move around from house to house.

8 "When you enter a town and are welcomed, eat what is offered to you. 9 Heal the sick who are there and tell them, 'The kingdom of God has come near to you.' 10 But when you enter a town and are not welcomed, go into its streets and say, 11 'Even the dust of your town we wipe from our feet as a warning to you. Yet be sure of this: The kingdom of God has come near.' *12 I tell you, it will be more bearable on that day for Sodom than for that town.*

13 "Woe to you, Chorazin! Woe to you, Bethsaida! For if the miracles that were performed in you had been performed in Tyre and Sidon, they would have repented long ago, sitting in sackcloth and ashes. 14 But it will be more bearable for Tyre and Sidon at the judgment than for you. 15 And you, Capernaum, will you be lifted to the heavens? No, you will go down to Hades.

16 "Whoever listens to you listens to me; whoever rejects you rejects me; but whoever rejects me rejects him who sent me."

17 The seventy-two returned with joy and said, "Lord, even the demons submit to us in your name."

18 He replied, "I saw Satan fall like lightning from heaven. 19 I have given you authority to trample on snakes and scorpions and to overcome all the power of the enemy; nothing will harm you. 20 However, do not rejoice that the spirits submit to you, but rejoice that your names are written in heaven."

21 At that time Jesus, full of joy through the Holy Spirit, said, "I praise you, Father, Lord of heaven and earth, because you have hidden these things from the wise and learned, and revealed them to little children. Yes, Father, for this is what you were pleased to do.

22 "All things have been committed to me by my Father. No one knows who the Son is except the Father, and no one knows who the Father is except the Son and those to whom the Son chooses to reveal him."

23 Then he turned to his disciples and said privately, "Blessed are the eyes that see what you see. 24 For I tell you that many prophets and kings wanted to see what you see but did not see it, and to hear what you hear but did not hear it."

Questions to Ponder

What has your perspective been on the nature of God's love? Do you see it as powerful?

Do you believe that love can change the minds of a whole town as it did in the story at the beginning of this chapter?

What areas of the world are you called to release God's love? The entertainment industry? The political realm? Families? The church?

Think of someone whose love gave them authority in your life. What kind of effect did they leave on you?

What kind of effect do you want your life to leave on others?

CHAPTER EIGHT

BECOMING LOVE

A few years ago I was visiting the capitol of Pakistan, Islamabad. My team and I ministered in several of the surrounding cities and saw amazing things happen. Paraplegics were healed, blind eyes were opened, tumors fell off, the presence of God followed us wherever we went. In fact, the presence had been so thick and the miracles so numerous at our last meeting that we had to be escorted out because so many people rushed the stage to get closer to where the presence of God was falling.

After we returned back to capitol, I called an old friend that lived in the city. He was a prominent leader in the Muslim community, and though we had obvious religious differences he had always respected the work I did and the honor with which I did it.

I was surprised when we arrived to meet with him. In the past he had always prepared the best food and been a vivacious host. This time he had only set out some tea and a few biscuits. I didn't mind of course, it was humbling to be treated so well. What bothered me was his downtrodden demeanor. He had none of his upbeat nature.

Finally, I could ignore it no longer and asked him what was wrong. He told me that he was sad because his son was in the hospital. There had been a problem with some of the lights during one of their events. His son climbed a ladder to try and fix the problem, but slipped when he was near the top. He landed badly, breaking his neck and becoming instantly paralyzed. He had been in a coma ever since, requiring a ventilator to breath. It was still unclear whether or not he would recover.

My heart went out to him. I tried to imagine how I would feel if the same thing had happened to my own son. A scripture came to mind. A scripture I had been mulling over for years and years. John 17:26

> *26 I have made you known to them, and will continue to make you known in order that the love you have for me may be in them and that I myself may be in them."*

It was part of a prayer that Jesus had spoken over all believers. It kept flowing through my mind again and again. What would happen if that love poured out on this family right now? What would that look like?

I didn't know, but I did know that we had to pray. Right away, the team and I lifted up prayers for the man's son. We prayed for his immediate healing. That he would not be paralyzed. That he would not need to be on a ventilator.

Everyone could feel the presence of God show up as we prayed, but afterwards that scripture continued to churn in my mind. I asked if it were possible for us to go to the hospital and pray for his son.

A few minutes later we were being escorted by armed guards to the hospital. Once we arrived I was told that I would be the only one able to go up to the room. So the rest of the team waited downstairs in the lobby as I went up to visit the young man.

Everything looked just as dire as the man had described. Dozens of tubes were coming out of different parts of the young man's body, he was hooked to several machines, and the atmosphere itself seemed to quench hope.

I prayed with everything I had. Immediately I felt the presence come as it so often had. Peace replaced despair. Hope replaced fear. I was certain that the love I felt stirring in my heart was about to be revealed in the body of this young man. I continued to pray for as long as the nurses allowed, feeling a continual increase of His presence, but seeing no external signs of healing. Then our time was up and I was escorted back to the lobby.

The man thanked me for praying for his son. He was grateful for the sense of hope that had been released as we prayed, as was I, but I couldn't help but feel that I had somehow missed something.

Later that evening, back at our hotel, I was resting with the team. I was partially vacant as we sat and ate together, thoughts of the young man running through my mind. We had seen so many healings just a few days before. Why should things be any different for this young man? And still that scripture kept cycling again and again in my mind. *That the love you have for me would be in them.*

I could feel that love. I felt it moving and shifting, hungry to be released on those people. *That the love you have for me would be in them.*

Then I suddenly heard the Lord ask me a question, "Leif, would you let your son be the one who is paralyzed? Would you have him be immobile, hooked to a ventilator, possibly for the rest of his life so that this young man could be well?"

It wasn't just a theoretical or theological question. The question He asked carried weight. I thought of my son, my only son. I thought of his sisters and his mother. How they would miss him. I thought of all the future we had ahead of us. I thought of the future children he would want to play ball with. And I felt just how much it would cost to give it all up.

It felt so real. If felt as though, if I spoke a few words, it would happen. My son would be sick and my friend's son would be well. I began to weep.

Finally I said, "Papa, I don't know how to love this way."

And immediately a love so powerful I could barely contain it came over me. My weeping turned into sobbing. The team turned and asked if I was alright. The feeling of love was so strong that I could hardly respond.

It was a love big enough for everyone. A love so complete that it held the answer for every question, the solution to every problem. I couldn't think of someone without the love leaping out of me and flooding toward them. I fell in love with my friend and his son. I fell in love with my family all over again. I fell in love with my team. And my love deepened for each of them.

The love was complete and whole. It didn't need anything back in return. It was good enough to just pour out the love again, again, and again.

Fifteen minutes later the phone rang and my coordinator answered.

It was my friend from earlier. He asked, "Where's Leif?"

My coordinator turned and looked at me and said, "He's right here," she answered, confused.

"No, no, no," he exclaimed over the phone, "I just saw him. He said he was going to the hospital. I called the hospital and they told me that my son no longer needs the ventilator."

I was stunned, but then I heard the voice of the Holy Spirit as clearly as I had ever heard it.

He said, "That was just one drop of the love that I have to give."

A Lasting Transformation

God is always looking for ways to reveal His love to us. Every time we see it, there is an opportunity to be transformed by it. He revealed the key to a scripture that had been on my heart for years through one miracle. I did not learn it through knowledge or by decoding a mystery. I learned it by experience.

The transformation that comes from an experience with God's love is always permanent. His love is not fleeting. It is not temporary. He gives it and does not take it away. He gives and keeps on giving. Every scripture, every miracle, every divine coincidence is a touch from heaven, reminding us of the love that He has given.

Since God's love can not be taken away, the enemy attacks it in other ways. He seeks to make our sensitivity to God's love grow dull.

If we want to make the transformation of love last in our lives then we must continually tune our hearts to His. To do this we must learn to feel every touch, hear every word, and see every move of his presence.

The same principle applies in marriage. If we, as married people, do not protect our love, it will grow stale. We can't afford to let "I love you," become nothing more than a casual phrase we say on our way out the door like "See you later," or "Have a nice day." We must work to keep our love sharp, to keep it honed, so that its meaning does not become dull.

How do you keep love fresh in a marriage? You buy each other gifts from time to time, write love notes, try new things together, share kind words, learn about each other's interests, and go on dates. Keeping our love fresh with God is not all that different.

Here are a few practical ways to help perpetuate the transformation of love that God is releasing in your life.

Pursue Prophecy. We are meant to eagerly desire the gift of the prophetic. Both the receiving and giving of it. They are the kind words of a loving father. A personal declaration of affection and encouragement. 1 Corinthians 14:1 says:

Follow the way of love and eagerly desire gifts of the Spirit, especially prophecy.

Each prophetic word you receive is not only a word for you, not just a piece of information, but a window into how God thinks of you. It is a love note from Him. Furthermore, every prophetic word you give is not only a word for that person, but a window into how God thinks about His people. Having a constant inflow and outflow of prophetic declaration gives us a regularly refreshed view of His heart.

Read The Word With Him. The Bible is God's sovereign word; a divine tapestry illustrating His pursuit of mankind, woven over thousands of years. The best part is that you get to read through every piece of that masterwork sitting with the one who inspired it. You get to ask Him questions, get His opinion on specific events, and feel what He felt as those things were happening. It should be obvious, but God was present at every event recorded in the Bible. He was there watching, working, guiding His children, and releasing His love just as He is today. Imagine all the wonderful things He has to tell you about the history of His love. And ask Him questions.

Once my wife asked my spiritual father, Jack Taylor, "Do you ever get perplexed when you read the Word?"

He replied, "More and more."

The Holy Spirit is with us to introduce answers and new mysteries through His word. It is a divine scavenger hunt for God's glory.

Go On Walks With Him. This may seem overly simple and practical, but I find a certain romantic charm in the idea of walking with God in the cool of the day as Adam and Eve did. Jesus has paid the price for our journey back to the Father's heart. Nothing is holding us back from Him. If we can boldly come to the throne of grace, then surely we can go on a walk with Him. Besides, a walk gives your body and mind just enough to do to keep it from being distracted. Not to mention it's good exercise.

Personal Application

Tuning our hearts to God is a daily process. Just like our bodies need food and rest, our spirit needs to be reconnected with our creator. So I am going to send you on a date with your Dad. First, say this simple prayer:

Father, I love you so much.
Thank you for loving me in return.
I want to protect my relationship with you.
Teach me how to tune my heart to yours every day.
Now I want to spend time with you.
Please tell me how you want to meet with me.

God is going to show you what kind of date He wants to take you on. It may be as simple as a walk through a beautiful place. He may want to go to dinner with you. He may just want to sit and talk with you in your home. Whatever it is, make sure to spend it focused on Him. He may tell you about your life or the lives of your loved ones. He may tell you secrets hidden in His Word. Or He may just say how much He loves you. Be ready for whatever He has for you.

Afterwards, read through the full version of the prayer that Jesus prayed over His disciples and believers at large. Imagine that He is praying every word over your life as you go forth, transforming the world with His love.

John 17:6-26

6 "I have revealed you to those whom you gave me out of the world. They were yours; you gave them to me and they have obeyed your word. 7 Now they know that everything you have given me comes from you. 8 For I gave them the words you gave me and they accepted them. They knew with certainty that I came from you, and they believed that you sent me. 9 I pray for them. I am not praying for the world, but for those you have given me, for they are yours. 10 All I have is yours, and all you have is mine. And glory has come to me through them. 11 I will remain in the world no longer, but they are still in the world, and I am coming to you. Holy Father, protect them by the power of your name, the name you gave me, so that they may be one as we are one. 12 While I was with them, I protected them and kept them safe by that name you gave me. None has been lost except the one doomed to destruction so that Scripture would be fulfilled.

13 "I am coming to you now, but I say these things while I am still in the world, so that they may have the full measure of my joy within them. 14 I have given them your word and the world has hated them, for they are not of the world any more than I am of the world. 15 My prayer is not that you take them out of the world but that you protect them from the evil one. 16 They are not of the world, even as I am not of it. 17 Sanctify them by the truth; your word is truth. 18 As you sent me into the world, I have sent them into the world. 19 For them I sanctify myself, that they too may be truly sanctified.

20 "My prayer is not for them alone. I pray also for those who will believe in me through their message, 21 that all of them may be one, Father, just as you are in me and I am in you. May they also be in us so that the world may believe that you have sent me. 22 I have given them the glory that you gave me, that they may be one as we are one— 23 I in them and you in me—so that they may be brought to complete unity. Then the world will know that you sent me and have loved them even as you have loved me.

24 "Father, I want those you have given me to be with me where I am, and to see my glory, the glory you have given me because you loved me before the creation of the world.

25 "Righteous Father, though the world does not know you, I know you, and they know that you have sent me. 26 I have made you known to them, and will continue to make you known in order that the love you have for me may be in them and that I myself may be in them

Questions to Ponder

What are some of the personal encounters you have had with God's love?

How has your life been different since that encounter?

What do you think you could do to tune your heart with God's heart every day?

What do you think your day to day would look like if you lived every moment connected to His heart?

CHAPTER NINE

TRANSFORMING LOVE

He picked his spot at the top of the hill carefully. He didn't want to be too close, that could be dangerous. But he definitely didn't want to be so far that he missed any of what happened, that wouldn't do at all. He finally decided on a spot just east of the city, the hills there afforded the best view without being within range of what was about to happen.

Looking up at where the sun sat in the sky, he judged that he still had another hour at least before things got started. He quickly gathered together a few loose pieces of wood and built himself a little shelter. It was hot work on this dry day and there wasn't much wood to be found, so his lean-to provided only a little shady relief from the hot sun.

But that was no longer the most important thing on his

mind. It would be any moment now. He sat hunched in his little hovel, eyes fixed on the city below.

It had been quite the journey getting to this point, but now he finally felt that it had all been worth it. He had run from his duty at first, and why shouldn't he? God had seen fit to send him to Nineveh. Nineveh! The same Nineveh that regularly raided his homeland, killing, raping, and plundering from his countrymen. Nineveh where every sin against God was committed in broad daylight.

He had given the word of God before. He knew what happened when the Lord spoke. There was repentance, restoration, even forgiveness. How could God, in His infinite wisdom, think that the people of Nineveh would ever turn from their disgusting ways? How could He dignify them with a warning? They were too evil, even for His graces.

His denial had done him no good, however. Attempting to escape the word of warning God had given him, he had hopped on a ship heading for Tarshish, firmly in the opposite direction of Nineveh. But God sent a storm, one so violent that even the experienced seamen on board feared for their lives. It was soon made clear that he was the reason for the storm. Then he was unceremoniously tossed overboard.

But that hadn't been the end of the indignity. God sent a fish to swallow him whole. Three days he had been in the fish. Three days God sustained him in the belly of that beast. Finally he had prayed and God heard him, causing the fish to vomit him up onto dry land.

What choice did he have then? He made his way to Nineveh. It took three days to walk every street in the city, declaring the impending judgment of the city. Forty days was the number God had given him, and now forty days it had been. He had delivered God's message and left to watch the judgment come to pass.

Atop his hill, with his makeshift shelter partially blocking the relentless sun, he waited and watched. Ready to see what method of destruction God would use put an end to the despicable city.

An hour passed, then another, and another. The sun was beating down on his head. He could feel the skin beginning to burn. He tried to wriggle down lower into his little shack, but it offered little relief. Still his eyes remained fixed on the city. Surely it would be any moment.

Another hour passed. No, he thought. It could not be. The people of Nineveh could not have changed their ways so quickly. There was no way they had repented. Even if they had, how could God actually forgive them. After all the horrible things they had done. How could the Lord be so foolish as to believe them.

The sun was beginning to set.

"Isn't this what I said, Lord, when I was still at home?" He shouted into the air, "That is why I tried to forestall by fleeing to Tarshish. I knew that you are a gracious and compassionate God," he kicked at the dirt, "slow to anger and abounding in love," he spat, "a God who relents from sending calamity."

He stood up and held his arms in the air, "Now Lord, take away my life, for it is better for me to die than to live."

The Lord replied in the ever patient and gentle tone He always did, "Is it right for you to be angry?"

He did not answer. Instead he stomped back to his little

shelter. There he watched the sun as it set.

That night a leafy plant grew up and around his little shelter, so that when he woke up in the morning there was plenty of shade. This made his little spot at the top of the hill that much more bearable. He assumed that this was God's way of apologizing for His mistake with Nineveh. He continued to watch and wait, hoping that the Lord would come to His senses about Nineveh as well. After all, whatever repentance the city had performed must have been undone by now. Surely they had returned to their sinning as soon as the day of judgment had past.

But the city survived the rest of that day, and he went to sleep in his shelter hoping that he would wake up to find the city burned to a crisp.

He woke up with the sun blazing down on his face. He turned abruptly and saw that the leafy plant that had provided so much comfort the day before had withered and died. What leaves were left had been chewed to bits by some kind of worm. The sun was beaming down, hotter than ever, while a stinging wind from the east pulled in even more heat from the desert.

As the heat began to make him feel faint, he leapt to his feet and shouted, "It would be better for me to die than to live."

Again, the peaceful voice of the Lord came, "Is it right for you to be angry about the plant?"

"It is," he said defiantly, "And I'm so angry I wish I were dead."

"You have been concerned about this plant," the Lord continued, "though you did not tend it or make it grow. It sprang up overnight and died overnight. And should I not have concern for the great city of Nineveh, in which there are more than a hundred and twenty thousand people who cannot tell their right hand from their left – and also many animals?"

To this, Jonah had no answer.

Tidal Waves of Love

Jonah is a classically tragic biblical figure. Despite all the clear opportunities to recognize the transformative work of love that God was trying to do in the city of Nineveh, he simply would not be moved. He thought his perspective was anointed, but it was just annoyed.

It is easy to understand Jonah's perspective. The Ninevites were a thorn in the side for anyone that crossed their path. They regularly carried out violent raids on neighboring cities, were known to instigate piracy along nearby trade routes, and were famous for their ritualistic idol worship. They were the Vikings of their time.

It is almost certain that Jonah, as a traveling prophet and preacher, would have seen the destruction caused by the people of Nineveh. He would have seen the orphaned children and ruined households that were left in their wake. It's fair to assume that he had good reason to hate Nineveh. Why else would he go to so much effort to avoid giving them an opportunity to repent?

It is God's desire that all nations and peoples come to

know Him. He is ready to release tidal waves of love that will sweep across every part of the world. This wave of love will sweep over the church, renewing our connection and identity in Him. But this wave will also sweep over the mosques, the Buddhist temples, the synagogues, the cultist compounds, and places of atheist study. It will sweep over the homeless, the wealthy, the ignorant and the educated. It will move through wall street. It will move through the republican and democratic parties. It will flood the slums of Southampton and saturate the streets of Beverly Hills. It will cover Bagdad, fill the Silicon Valley, and overtake the city of Moscow. It will bring love, hope, and transformation wherever it goes.

While we might understand the decision that Jonah made, we also have to remember that none of us deserve the grace we have received. The story of Jonah is made tragic because, in it, the wicked city of Nineveh is transformed by the loving correction of a merciful God while the man of God sent to release His word is not.

Let us avoid the trap that ensnared Jonah by never being offended by where God chooses to pour out His Spirit. How do we steward the restoration of a known terrorist? How do we respond when a thief who has stolen the livelihood of thousands asks for forgiveness? What do we do with the murderer, the rapist, the racist when God's love turns their heart? I might not know my reaction, but I know my God. I also pray that my reaction will match His.

It is as Jonah said. Our God is gracious and compassionate, slow to anger and abounding in love. I do not know how to show love to everyone in the world yet, but I am willing to let my Father show me how.

Jennifer, the children, and I moved back to America from Norway to work at a local church. We were excited to see what God was going to do in the lives of the people we loved in that congregation. Before long, we realized that the lessons the Lord was teaching us about the move of the Spirit were neither accepted or wanted in our church.

They struggled with the gifts of the Spirit, the gift of tongues, healing, prophetic words and all that Jesus promised for believers. Slowly but surely we were pushed out of the church.

We were sad, angry, hurt, but within a short amount of time we realized that the church letting us go was the perfect impetus to move into full-time ministry and total dependence on God. Before long that church ended up dissolving almost completely. I was surprised to find that I felt much greater sorrow at the church's demise than when they asked us to go.

God is ready to teach all of us to truly love our enemies, so that even when calamity falls on them we can be intercessors for their restoration.

Step One

If Jonah is one of the worst examples of how to partner with the transformation of God's love, then I believe that Daniel is one of the best. Daniel was captured at a young age and taken to be a servant in Babylon. He was forced into the service of a wicked king – a king who openly served false gods. He was denied any say in his future. He was given a pagan name. Everything was taken from him.

Daniel had every right to be angry with his lot in life. He certainly had every right to be angry at the king who had committed this injustice. Yet, he instead chose to serve Nebuchadnezzar with dignity and honor.

This did not mean that Daniel would compromise his core values. When the men in charge of him demanded that he eat ceremonially unclean food, Daniel created a solution. He did not whine or complain. He negotiated a reasonable bargain with honor and grace.

The part that impresses me most about Daniel is that he actually came to love the man who took everything from him. This was not a false love or even the obligatory love that all children of God are required to show. He showed genuine care for Nebuchadnezzar's well being. In Daniel 9:19, Daniel was in the middle of interpreting a dream for Nebuchadnezzar:

> *19 Then Daniel (also called Belteshazzar) was greatly perplexed for a time, and his thoughts terrified him. So the king said, "Belteshazzar, do not let the dream or its meaning alarm you."*
>
> *Belteshazzar answered, "My lord, if only the dream applied to your enemies and its meaning to your adversaries!*

Nebuchadnezzar received a dream of judgment from God and, rather than celebrating the potential downfall of his oppressor, Daniel laments at the news saying, "if only the dream applied to your enemies." This was a wicked king. This was the man that tried to burn Daniel's friends in a furnace because they wouldn't worship an idol. This was the man who had oppressed Israel for years. Daniel should have been glad that Nebuchadnezzar was getting what he deserved, but the honor he had for the king was too great.

Daniel went on to serve several leaders and he showed the same grace to each, honoring every one to the best of his ability, even when they did not show the same honor in return. If we want to have the same impact that Daniel had in the kingdom of Babylon, then we need to learn how to honor the way he did.

We need to stop dishonoring our governmental leaders. If we believe the Word of God, He sets up kings and leaders. We need to ask God how to bring forth the changes He wants to see. We need to stop acting out of fear when facing the threats of terrorists. We need to start seeing criminals through the eyes of heaven's justice rather than the spirit of vengeance. We also must not compromise, just as Daniel did not compromise himself to accommodate the king. It is a delicate balance to walk, but each of us have the Holy spirit as a guide.

Step one to releasing the wave of love that is ready to sweep the entire world is learning to honor. Honor is the foundation of revival. It is the solid ground where the building blocks of heaven can be laid on earth. If we can learn to honor anyone, we can learn to love anyone. If we can love anyone, we can change the world.

Personal Application

It is not always easy to learn how to honor. It doesn't come cheap. Honor almost always costs something, and it is usually things more valuable than money. The best way I know how to expand my capacity for honor is to be inspired by the ones who carry it well, and there are few who carry it better than David.

Below I have included a very interesting story that happened between King Saul and David. This was during the time when Saul had been hunting David. David had been hiding out in caves and running for his life from place to place. Saul had gone mad, trying to kill David for almost no reason.

David had every right to hate Saul. In this story, David passes up an opportunity to kill Saul. He takes a token to prove the encounter had happened, but David's capacity for honor is so great that even that small gesture makes him feel convicted. Watch how David's honor for a dishonorable man releases transformation. As you read be thinking of the people in your own life that you have a hard time honoring, and ask the Holy Spirit to show you how to display the same honor that David gave to Saul.

1 Samuel 24:1-22

> *1 After Saul returned from pursuing the Philistines, he was told, "David is in the Desert of En Gedi." 2 So Saul took three thousand able young*

men from all Israel and set out to look for David and his men near the Crags of the Wild Goats.

3 He came to the sheep pens along the way; a cave was there, and Saul went in to relieve himself. David and his men were far back in the cave. *4* The men said, "This is the day the LORD spoke of when he said to you, 'I will give your enemy into your hands for you to deal with as you wish.'" Then David crept up unnoticed and cut off a corner of Saul's robe.

5 Afterward, David was conscience-stricken for having cut off a corner of his robe. *6* He said to his men, "The LORD forbid that I should do such a thing to my master, the LORD's anointed, or lay my hand on him; for he is the anointed of the LORD." *7* With these words David sharply rebuked his men and did not allow them to attack Saul. And Saul left the cave and went his way.

8 Then David went out of the cave and called out to Saul, "My lord the king!" When Saul looked behind him, David bowed down and prostrated himself with his face to the ground. *9* He said to Saul, "Why do you listen when men say, 'David is bent on harming you'? *10* This day you have seen with your own eyes how the LORD delivered you into my hands in the cave. Some urged me to kill you, but I spared you; I said, 'I will not lay my hand on my lord, because he is the LORD's anointed.' *11* See, my father, look at this piece of your robe in my hand! I cut off the corner of your robe but did not kill *you. See that there is nothing in my hand to indicate that I am guilty of wrongdoing or rebellion. I have not wronged you, but you are hunting me down to take my life. 12 May the LORD judge between you and me. And may the LORD avenge the wrongs you have done to me, but my hand will not touch you. 13 As the old saying goes, 'From evildoers come evil deeds,' so my hand will not touch you.*

14 *"Against whom has the king of Israel come out? Who are you pursuing? A dead dog? A flea? 15 May the LORD be our judge and decide between us. May he consider my cause and uphold it; may he vindicate me by delivering me from your hand."*

16 *When David finished saying this, Saul asked, "Is that your voice, David my son?" And he wept aloud. 17 "You are more righteous than I," he said. "You have treated me well, but I have treated you badly. 18 You have just now told me about the good you did to me; the LORD delivered me into your hands, but you did not kill me. 19 When a man finds his enemy, does he let him get away unharmed? May the LORD reward you well for the way you treated me today. 20 I know that you will surely be king and that the kingdom of Israel will be established in your hands. 21 Now swear to me by the LORD that you will not kill off my descendants or wipe out my name from my father's family."*

22 So David gave his oath to Saul. Then Saul re-turned home, but David and his men went up to the stronghold.

Questions to Ponder

Are there any people, groups, or social classes that you have hard time giving honor?

Can you believe that God is willing to forgive and bring transformation to those people or groups?

How could you be a key player in bringing God's love to those people or groups?

What is your part in bringing the tidal wave of love that God is ready to sweep across the world?

It's up to you!

John 17:26

> *And I have declared to them Your name, and*
> *will declare it, that the love with which You*
> *loved Me may be in them, and I in them.*

This verse is the heart and soul of this work. There is no way that I can bring forth any change in your heart or life, but I know the one who can. He is so willing and able to release His spirit in you because He is so in love with you. He is a good, good Father. God will give you every good thing. Jesus prayed that the PERFECT love of the Father would be in us. All we have to do is receive it, then we cannot fail! Ask the Father to help you receive what you cannot achieve:

TRANSFORMING LOVE!

AVAILABLE NOW FROM LEIF HETLAND:

Seeing Through Heaven's Eyes

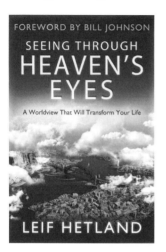

A worldview that will transform your life...This beautifully written memoir-essay explores the realities of Papa God's love for you, your destiny as His beloved child and heir, and the transformation of your vision of yourself, others, and world events that this revelation of your place in the divine family brings.

Available in Hardback and Paperback

Healing the Orphan Spirit

All that the Father has is ours! All creation is groaning for the sons and daughters to be revealed. It is time for us to come into the fullness of who we were created to be so all creation will come back to the Father's house.

Available in Paperback and Ebook

The Power of Shalom

The Hebrew word "Shalom" is often described as Peace, but it entails so much more. What is the level of peace that we live in today, that we are laying a foundation for the next generation? Listen to Leif as he discusses Shalom! And of course, "May peace, completeness, and wholeness be upon you…"

Available in MP3 and CD

Which Chair Are You Sitting In?

One of Leif's most popular messages! All of us operate from one of three chairs: Commitment, Compromise or Conflict. Learn where you are and how to stay in Chair #1.

Available in MP3 and CD

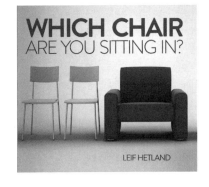

For more information on our upcoming conferences, international ministry trips, or to purchase books, eBooks, mp3s, CDs or DVDs from our web store, please visit our website at:

globalmissionawareness.com

PO Box 3049, Peachtree City, GA, 30269

770.487.4800